C0-CBY-758

OPERATIONAL RISK

Operational Risk

The New Challenge for Banks

Gerrit Jan van den Brink

368.1
B85o

Language translations copyright © 2002 by Palgrave Publishers Ltd
Operational Risk copyright © 2002 by Schäffer-Poeschel Verlag GMbH & Co. KG
All rights reserved.
Published by arrangement with Schäffer-Poeschel Verlag GMbH

All rights reserved. No reproduction, copy or transmission of this publication may be made without written permission.

No paragraph of this publication may be reproduced, copied or transmitted save with written permission or in accordance with the provisions of the Copyright, Designs and Patents Act 1988, or under the terms of any licence permitting limited copying issued by the Copyright Licensing Agency, 90 Tottenham Court Road, London W1T 4LP.

Any person who does any unauthorized act in relation to this publication may be liable to criminal prosecution and civil claims for damages.

The author has asserted his right to be identified as the author of this work in accordance with the Copyright, Designs and Patents Act 1988.

First published 2002 by
PALGRAVE
Houndmills, Basingstoke, Hampshire RG21 6XS and
175 Fifth Avenue, New York, N.Y. 10010
Companies and representatives throughout the world

PALGRAVE is the new global academic imprint of St. Martin's Press LLC Scholarly and Reference Division and Palgrave Publishers Ltd (formerly Macmillan Press Ltd).

ISBN 0–333–96868–9

This book is printed on paper suitable for recycling and made from fully managed and sustained forest sources.

A catalogue record for this book is available from the British Library.

Library of Congress Cataloging-in-Publication Data

Brink, Gerrit Jan van den, 1968-
Operational risk : the new challenge for banks / Gerrit Jan van den Brink.
p. cm.
Includes bibliographical references and index.
ISBN 0-333-96868-9
1. Bank management. 2. Risk management. I. Title.

HG1615 .B75 2001
368.1'068'1–dc21 2001036528

10 9 8 7 6 5 4 3 2 1
11 10 09 08 07 06 05 04 03 02

Printed and bound in Great Britain by
Antony Rowe Ltd, Chippenham, Wiltshire

To Simone

University Libraries
Carnegie Mellon University
Pittsburgh, PA 15213-3890

Contents

List of Tables

List of Figures

Acknowledgements

The desire to write a practice-oriented book regarding operational risk has become a reality with the completion of this work. This book was originally written in German, but I was encouraged by Frank Katzenmayer, who assisted me with the German publication with Schäffer-Poeschel-Verlag, to translate this book into English.

After a couple of months translating I am grateful to have the opportunity to publish this book in English, which is actualized in accordance with the consultative paper of the Basle Committee for Banking Supervision. It will hopefully place the ideas discussed before a much larger public, and equally importantly bring those ideas to the attention of experts in the Netherlands also. Although I have been living in Germany for more than five years now, I still feel a strong bond to my country of origin.

I am grateful to Palgrave who have given me the opportunity to publish in English. Also, this book could not have been completed without the moral support of my wife Simone, who, with my daughter Laura, had to miss me for many hours, even in difficult times; I am grateful to them both that they enabled me to concentrate on this work for such long periods.

Königstein im Taunus   GERRIT JAN VAN DEN BRINK

Introduction

Operational risk has been perceived as an important theme for financial institutions only relatively recently. Sometimes operational risk has been seen as a market risk (as in the early days after the Barings case), or as a credit risk (as in the case of Jürgen Schneider in Germany), both of which turned out to be wrong judgements at a later stage. Barings Bank did not face a market risk, since the unauthorized high futures position resulted in a considerable loss and not the unexpected market movements. In the credit loss case of Jürgen Schneider, banks were granting credits although they were aware of problems with the creditworthiness of this customer.

These well-known losses lie within the range US $400–2850 million. However, these losses are only a small part of the total loss volume of institutions, since most losses are too small to deserve public attention and financial institutions have no interest in making this information more widely known. The publication of such information could have negative influences on the trust relationship between customers and the financial institutions. These amounts, however, show the need for a proper operational risk management strategy and involvement of regulators as well.

Moreover, losses have also been caused by computer viruses such as the 'I love you' virus in 2000. Even secure systems were infected and losses in Europe and the United States amounted to billions of dollars. The impact of progress made in the electronic era is also becoming clear: the benefits of the new distribution channel, the Internet, are clear, but it has a negative counter-side. Criminal activities may damage not only the systems of financial institutions, but their reputations. Internet banking is promoted as secure by financial institutions, but virus problems are demonstrating that security is not as adequate as clients have been told.

Recent decades have been characterized by change, and the following changes have had a big impact on the banking industry:

- Deregulation
- Globalization
- Complex products
- The Internet as a new distribution channel

Deregulation started in the 1970s as the Bretton Woods agreement became obsolete. Until then the relationships between foreign currencies were quite stable through gold parity. After the end of the Bretton Woods agreement, the prices of currencies became market-driven causing more volatility in rates of exchange.

Money and capital markets were deregulated, and in the 1980s near-banking became normalized. Commercial paper and medium-term notes were introduced to markets eroding the role of financial institutions as intermediaries. Derivatives were introduced to the markets, and financial institutions used the derivatives to gain more flexibility in their management of market risks and later for credit risk management as well. Although these products were originally intended to hedge market risks, suddenly they were used to speculate as well. The products allow considerable positions to be taken without investing the corresponding liquidity in cash instruments. The cost of carrying such positions is therefore considerably lower, and it is clear that, especially in the early days, the risks were not always completely understood by senior management. Many of the losses mentioned earlier relate to trading with derivative products.

Globalization not only affects the competitive position of financial institutions, it opens markets for competitors who were not previously players in the local markets. Cross-subsidizing becomes a real danger to the existence of a financial institution, since players who are specialized in a product, which is contributing and subsidizing other products within the financial institution concerned, will beat the more expensive product out of the market. The financial institution is then condemned to exercise tight cost-reduction programmes, which will also introduce new operational risks.

Another relevant point is culture, which is an important basis for trust. Sometimes internal control measures which are quite effective in Europe and North America will fail in other parts of the world, since they do not fit with the local culture. It may be surprising to learn that in Indonesia it is not the practice to give one staff member the code of the safe and another staff member the key; a procedure which is very common in both Europe and North America. In Indonesia, staff members who do not have the key or the code feel mistrusted by senior management. Everybody in the department should know the code and where the key is stored. As soon as money disappears, the group itself will discover the person who acted dishonestly, since the honour of the whole group is at stake.

The same is true for management. In some countries it is not done to say 'no' to senior management or staff members from headquarters, even if the requested action is impossible or will result in negative outcomes. This attitude is a powerful cause of operational risk if it is not recognized by staff members from head office or senior management.

Culture is also important in the relationship between management and staff members. In Western Europe itself, some citizens communicate quite directly and openly, whilst others communicate diplomatically. In Asia communication needs to be conducted in such a way that nobody loses face. If a key staff member is losing face, he is forced to resign. If the manager originates from a culture in which more direct communication is common, he may be embarrassed when confronted with the resignation of this staff member.

On the other hand, customers expect a global relationship management of their account and require the same quality globally. But due to different approaches in various countries, it may be hard to guarantee the same quality around the globe.

Globalization has also had effects on financial institutions' operations. It became quite common during the 1990s to concentrate operations in one location per time zone, and for some products a global processing centre was chosen. Due to time-zone issues these centres had to work in shifts, and systems no longer had the night time for batch processing. In most main processing systems it is still impossible to run batch jobs – for example interest calculations and accounting operations – while the on-line activities are active. The small window available causes problems since the repair time available after process disturbances is quite small, and the information or the system itself may be available too late, causing operational risks.

Due to the introduction of derivatives, *product complexity* has also increased, so that it is more difficult to perceive and analyse the inherent risks. If these risks are not properly understood, risk control will not function effectively; risks may be either completely overseen or inadequately measured and reported. Both issues may result in wrong decisions. Product complexity is also an issue in the case of processing, since processing systems have not developed as quickly as structured products. These products have to be decomposed into basic products which are then processed in the 'old' processing systems. As a consequence, the confirmation has to be processed manually. It is clear that this error source should not be overlooked. In 'unwinding' such a product, one of the basic products may be easily forgotten, and at this moment the financial institution reports wrong positions internally and also in the regulatory information.

The last theme to be discussed is the *internet as a distribution channel*. The internet was originally meant as a knowledge-exchange network between universities and nobody had expected such a tremendous paradigm change regarding its use. Now it is used by many organizations and individuals and there is no control institution in the network. There are also criminal activities on the internet. Due to the on-line banking feature banks had to open their systems to allow an internet connection, and even after the implementation of security measures the door is still not completely closed.

Firewalls may be useful as virus scans are common. The big risk, however, is not located at the bank's site, but at the customer's site. MS Windows is an open house into which everybody can have a look as long as the PC is connected to the internet. If a smart card is still active, third parties may be allowed to set up an authenticated communication session with the financial institution and act as though they were the customer of the bank.

Another point of misuse concerns frames within the internet pages of financial institutions. Criminals may ask the customer to enter credit card details while the customer believes he is communicating with the bank only. The customer may later be embarrassed to see huge amounts charged to his account by the credit card company.

The above-mentioned developments have required adaptations to be made by financial institutions. Changes contain inherent operational risks, but if the necessary changes are not implemented even larger operational risks may exist. Therefore operational risk management is seen as an integral part of the measures to protect financial institutions against excessive losses. Regulators have acknowledged the importance of adequate operational risk management strategies and the Basle Committee on Supervision has presented a consultative paper regarding the solvency requirements regarding such risks; the contents of that paper will be discussed in this book.

Financial institutions will not only try to optimize the regulatory capital charge as presented by the Basle Committee, but also to manage and control the operational risks to which they are exposed. In the coming chapters operational risk and its various dimensions, risk identification and quantification, and last but not least management alternatives, will be discussed. The discussion of scientific and practical progress has not yet been completed; this book is a contribution to an ongoing discussion which will, I hope, clarify both areas.

1 Definition and Dimensions of Operational Risk

DEFINITION AND CLASSIFICATION OF RISK

A generally accepted definition of operational risk in the banking sector is still not available at this moment; however, the most widely used definitions will be discussed in this chapter. Apart from having an agreed definition, each banking institute should define operational risk in a manner well-suited to its own situation and activities. A generally accepted definition should be available as soon as the Basle Committee formulates obligatory solvency requirements regarding operational risk.

The various parts of a bank's own definition mainly depend on the bank's activities. A transaction-oriented bank will probably stress the system dimension more than a relationship-oriented bank might. Example 1.1 considers the role that IT systems play in a direct bank (which mainly uses call centres and the internet as distribution channels).

Example 1.1

Transaction processing is highly automated in most banks. This is especially so for direct banks where transactions are directly fed from the front-office system into the back-office system by interfaces.

If the back-office system collapses, transactions from the front-office system may be lost (especially in the case of broadcasting techniques). It is therefore necessary to store transaction data temporarily. The complete arrival at the back-office system side is checked by using a loop to the front-office system. In the old legacy systems, some buffers sometimes simply overflow; non-recorded transactions are then lost without any warning.

Banks may be liable if customer transactions are not processed or are processed too late. Security transactions especially are vulnerable. The management of a direct bank will therefore pay a great deal of attention to the systems risk.

The two most widely used definitions for operational risk originate from the Group of 30 and the Basle Committee. The definition of the Group of 30[1] is:

> *The risk of losses occurring as a result of inadequate systems and control, human error, or management failure.*

Three dimensions of operational risk are mentioned in this definition: people, systems and procedures. The separate declaration of management failures is interesting. The Group of 30 sees management as a determining factor for the prevention of operational risk. Firstly, management is seen as an example for a control-oriented organization; it should guard the company's culture and provide living examples regarding the prevention of operational risk.

In 1992 the COSO report[2] was published in the USA, in which the control pyramid is described. The base of the pyramid (Figure 1.1) is the control environment, understood as a cultural part which means a control-oriented culture (positively seen) to prevent operational risk. Management is responsible for maintaining such a culture in the organization.

The Basle Committee defines operational risk as:

> *The risk of direct or indirect loss resulting from inadequate or failed internal processes, people and systems or from external events.*

This definition has an operational scope. The internal processes include both the procedure itself and the embedded internal controls. Inadequate

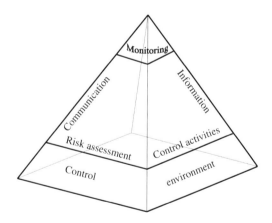

Figure 1.1   The control environment

Source: Committee of Sponsoring Organizations of the Treadway Commission (COSO) Jersey City, 1992.

Example 1.2

The data-entry procedure for fixed data in a back-office system is so designed that each staff member is able to change the customer's name, address and place. A verification by other colleagues is not necessary. Such a design error may not cause direct damage to the bank; although the customer will probably be irritated if he perceives that his name has been misspelt.

If the payment process is so designed that verification by another staff member is not necessary, the bank is exposed to an acute risk. Individual staff members could redirect payment orders to other accounts in order to benefit personally.

---

internal controls, however, cause an acute risk. Missing or inappropriate internal controls can be compared to an open door, while nobody is at home; one should not be surprised if valuables are stolen if no prevention measures are taken. The difference between inadequate procedures and internal controls is explained in Example 1.2.

Both definitions declare human error as an important dimension without any further distinction. However, there is a difference according to whether errors are executed with full awareness or not. In the first case, such errors should be categorized as fraud; the others can be classified as errors. The difference between market risk and operational risk is the impossibility of a bank gaining from operational risk. The bank may only lose if internal control weaknesses are used for their own interest by employees. Therefore – in our opinion – the distinction between fraud and errors is quite important for the analysis of operational risk.

Operational risk consists of the dimensions shown in Figure 1.2. The relationships between these various dimensions will be discussed explicitly in this chapter; the themes 'risk mitigation' and 'damage control' will be analysed in detail and the risks described.

Damage may be of different kinds. *Financial* damage normally occurs directly or shortly after an acute risk becomes perceivable and has a direct visible influence on the profit and loss account of the bank. For example, if payments are credited to the account of a person conducting fraud, the receiving bank is not allowed to redirect the payment, which was transferred correctly, as soon as the money has been credited to the account of the payee. If the money is withdrawn, the paying party only has the possibility of booking the amount as a loss.

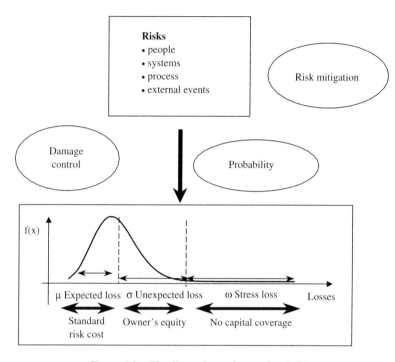

Figure 1.2   The dimensions of operational risk

Reputation damage has other features, and such damage cannot easily be recorded; in fact in some situations the bank will never know that it has suffered a reputation loss. Two types of reputation loss can be mentioned:

- loss of customers, caused by errors made by the bank; and
- loss of potential clients, who will not enter into a relationship with the bank due to negative information.

In the first case it is not only clients directly affected by the error that are meant; if such errors become known in the market, the bank must also consider that other clients may lose their trust in the bank and therefore quit the relationship.

The amount of a reputation loss may be far higher than for a financial loss. According to the theory of opportunity losses, the present value of all future cash flows regarding lost clients should be taken as the loss. If for example a term loan of US$1 000 000 over 30 years which has a margin of 1 per cent fails, the present value (which represents the loss) for the bank will be US $153 724.51 (the interest margin discounted against a rate of 5 per cent). It is evident that the loss of potential clients is especially hard to record. The bank might possibly take the development of its market share as an indicator, although many other influences affect the market share as well.

DIMENSIONS OF OPERATIONAL RISK

The Risks

In order to be able to quantify the various risk factors, these factors first need to be categorized. The main classes are:

- People
- Systems
- Procedures
- External risks

People

The operational risks regarding people can be classified as follows:

- Concentration problems, which may have very different causes.
- Overtime, which may be caused by qualitative or quantitative understaffing.
- Insufficient knowledge of products and/or procedures.
- Fraud by employees.

Nobody is perfect. Whether we like it or not, sometimes we forget something. Moreover, people are sometimes unable to draw clear boundaries between their business and private lives. Mostly the converse is true: since people do not discuss their private problems at work, such problems may not even be discovered. For example a death or the loss of a family member may cause that employee to be unable to concentrate on their work as under normal circumstances. The stress may even increase since the employee may wish to avoid being seen in a negative light. The employee may work hard to avoid further errors, but such behaviour will paradoxically result in even more errors.

Managers who are working in a culture in which business and private lives are separated should be sensitive to such employee behaviour. They should not try to change the culture, since that would take many years. They should be sensitive to the signals which mainly come through non-verbal communication, and in order to avoid a higher number of errors they may decide to reallocate team activities to take some pressure off the staff member concerned. This will relieve some of the stress and the employee will be able to concentrate better on the remaining activities.

Another evident source of errors is structural overtime. In the long run there is a price to pay for overtime; it may result in more frequent illness and a higher quota of errors of employees.

Products and procedures have become more and more complex in recent years; today it is hardly possible to know all banking products and procedures in detail. If knowledge of these fails, three different patterns of behaviour may result:

- The employee does not recognize that important knowledge is lacking and executes his tasks – although he believes he acts correctly – possibly wrongly.
- The employee recognizes that important knowledge is lacking, but it is uncomfortable to explain that he is not familiar with the task or situation.
- The employee recognizes the lack of important knowledge and tries to take advantage of that lack.

In the first two cases the employee will execute the tasks in a way he thinks is correct. This danger exists especially in the trading area where product features change more often. If these changes are not recognized, the bank may be confronted with claims and the loss of reputation. In some areas it is quite difficult to repair errors. For example, if a syndication manager makes errors, the market will recognize and remember; that bank will not be able to play the syndication manager's role in the future. Managers should therefore make sure that their employees are qualified for their jobs, and it should be recognized that the requirements for banking employees change frequently.

The last category to be discussed is fraud. With fraud, damage will always occur, and if a fraud case becomes public the reputation of the bank will be damaged as well. Banking business is based on trust between the customer and the bank; this trust relationship will be affected if a fraud case becomes publicly known.

Fraud cases are more likely to occur if internal procedures do not correspond to reality. This is especially so in the case of missing, wrongly-implemented or passed internal control measures when fraud may be stimulated. For example in a matrix organization one management level may trust that another level will take certain measures. If both management

---

Example 1.3 The matrix organization

Many international banks are organized as matrix organizations with a regional and a functional level. The regional level represents the normal hierarchical structure. The functional level is often product-oriented. Such organizational structures may cause confusion regarding responsibilities. The functional level of management may expect that the regional manager will solve known problems, whereas the regional manager thinks the same regarding the functional manager. Both managers may not see a need to communicate with each other regarding problems since for each of them it seems clear that the other will take appropriate action. As a result, no corrective actions are taken and the financial institution appears to lack control, although the process design itself is not the cause.

---

levels have the same thoughts, nothing will happen. Example 1.3 shows what the result of ill-based trust can be.

Managers should be able to recognize the triggers which motivate people to commit fraud, such as the following:

- Money
- Prestige
- Fun

If employees have financial problems, they are endangered. It may therefore be a better solution for a bank to support such employees in an adequate manner than to ignore the problem. Prestige is a dangerous motivator. Employees may participate in fraud because they are unable to maintain a certain social status. For such staff it is often the lesser evil to conduct fraud than to give up that status. Research[3] regarding fraud shows that employees can also conduct fraud just for fun. They consider the 'adrenalin-kick' as a positive.

Managers should be able to recognize patterns of behaviour of their employees which may potentially relate to, or lead to, fraud. They should improve the known weaknesses in their internal controls and they should make clear by their own behaviour that fraud will definitely not be tolerated in the organization. Nothing may be so damaging for an organization as management that does not behave in conformity with the organization's policies.

Systems

The risks concerning information systems can be classified as follows:

- General risks
- Application-oriented risks
- User-oriented risks

The general risks can be disaggregated into:

- Physical access to the hardware
- Logical access to the IT systems
- Change management
- Capacity management
- Emergency management
- Insufficient backup recovery measures

Physical access to the hardware sometimes means logical access to the systems as well. Some consoles of legacy systems are not password-protected, so that all users may execute system administrator's rights. In such a situation the manipulation of system procedures and data is possible. Even staff members with insufficient knowledge may disturb or terminate system procedures. Moreover, unauthorized staff have the possibility of writing data to external devices, which can be used outside the bank. If customer data become known outside the bank, the trust relationship between customer and bank may be negatively affected.

Logical access to systems and applications is of particular interest in the e-commerce era. Before the outbound connection system, boundaries were limited to the enterprise itself. The outbound connection, however, enables third parties to access the bank's systems without any physical presence. In this way hackers have already made confidential information of banks publicly known in some cases.

It would be wrong, however, to direct attention to the outside world only. Most incidents originate inside banking organizations. The most vulnerable area is collaboration, which disables the segregation of duties. Segregation of duties will itself be discussed in detail later in Chapter 3 (p. 95 ff). The purpose of segregating duties is to improve data quality. Therefore the entry of fixed and variable data is segregated in banks to avoid, for example, a situation where customers may be entered into the system who do not really exist. If such customers are recorded, it would be easy to close vague deals of which only staff may benefit.

Beside segregation of duties, dual control also exists. Segregation of duties deals with various activities which are not executed by the same employee, whereas in the case of dual control the same task is executed by two employees. The verification of data entries is a good example: the second employee verifies the entered data visually or by re-keying. The application itself controls whether the first entry matches the second in the case of key-verification. However, both the segregation of duties and dual control will be ineffective if the logical access to systems is not arranged adequately.

Change management procedures should guarantee that system functionality and existing data are not affected by the implementation of a new application or a new software version. Practically speaking, small errors often cause big errors. For example, if the lock function for cheques fails, high losses for the bank may be a consequence, although the error in itself is small.

Another source of errors is parallel local and central software development. In this case local software may be disabled if a new central version is implemented, and vice versa. The practical problems are displayed in Example 1.4.

Today, interfaces between systems are often used, and these interfaces may no longer function perfectly if changes have been implemented in the source or the target system. A good system of change management tries to detect in which parts of the software changes may have consequences. The expected consequences will then be addressed very carefully in the test plan.

Capacity management will try to prevent bottlenecks in all relevant system components. The problem may lie in the network, the internal memory, external memory or the database size itself. It these capacities are insufficient, processes may slow down or even be terminated. Imagine what would happen if the Reuters triarch system in a bank were to collapse: immediately traders would not be supplied with actual market data and the bank itself would not be able to display its own data on the Reuters sites any more. If the market turns out to be very volatile at that moment, the bank may be forced to charge the losses to the profit and loss account.

Much attention has been paid to *emergency planning* at all management levels, driven by the millennium problem. Many regulatory institutions inquired of banks regarding the prevention measures taken, and pointed out the importance of having adequate and tested emergency plans. Other calamities in the recent past have been the fire in Credit Lyonais Bank's headquarters and the explosion in the London financial district. In such emergencies the most vital processes in the bank may collapse; the resulting losses, but also the reputation losses, are hard to quantify.

Example 1.4 Change management and common systems

Many banks use global common systems for their branches and subsidiaries. Cost saving is a widely used argument, since the system has to be designed only once, and development and maintenance can be executed centrally. Nevertheless, generally accepted accounting principles and regulatory requirements vary in many countries and, moreover, each country has its own interfaces to exchanges, clearing houses and domestic payment systems. The global version has to be modified based on these local requirements, and such modifications are normally accompanied by high costs. Time pressure is also high during the implementation, as in the past with the introduction of the euro and the unavoidable millennium. It is clear that the documentation of changes may suffer under such circumstances.

As soon as a new global release has been installed, the local changes have to be reinstalled as well. The global version should therefore be accompanied by extensive documentation of changes and new features to enable local IT management to assess whether the local modifications will still function after the installation of the new release.

After the installation of the new global release and the reinstallation of the local modifications, the system should be thoroughly tested. The departments involved check the results, the screens and the system functionality; when satisfied, they will release the new system. In practice, however, such test procedures are mostly not followed. Damages caused by poor testing are mostly higher than the costs of orderly testing.

Backup recovery procedures should mitigate the consequences of system failures. For example, systems may be implemented and mirrored in such a way that in a critical incident they can be changed between the production and the backup machine. An important requirement is that both machines are configured in exactly the same manner and the IP addresses should be interchangeable. Otherwise the interfaces with other systems would not function anymore.

Application-oriented risks affect the quality of the processed information directly. Particular attention should be paid to the following errors:

- Data are not (correctly) recorded due to system errors.
- Data are not correctly stored during the period of their validity (integrity of data is not guaranteed).

- Relevant data are not (correctly) included in reports or irrelevant data are included.
- Calculations which are the basis for information are not correct.
- Due to system failures the information processed by the application is not available in time.

System errors may cause an incorrect completion of a database transaction. Normally such a transaction is reversed automatically, but in some cases the reversion does not function correctly. Another example is an inappropriate verification function: data are entered twice, but both entries are not matched correctly. During the valid period of the data, their integrity may be lost because of hardware errors (certain sectors on the hard disk are not readable), or because data are unauthorizedly overwritten by other data entries. 'Deadly embrace' is a frequent cause: two users access the same record at the same time; if the system does not prevent a double access, only the last change is saved. The first change will be lost, and the loss is not recognized.

The danger that all relevant data are not, or not correctly, included in reports increases if the inquiry is hard-coded in the software. If a new product is introduced, the necessary change in the software code is forgotten and the information will consequently be incomplete. If the inquiry was not coded correctly, data may be mixed: for example if currency fields are not correctly queried, a mixed number may be produced which is meaningless.

Incorrect calculations may have different causes; they may be due to a wrong interpretation of the functional specification, but also simply a programming error.

The last danger has a different nature: information is complete and correct, but it is delivered too late. Correct information about a bankrupt debtor will not help the bank in decision-making. Another example is the market information supply for a trader: as soon as the information flow is disturbed, the trader is not able to hedge his positions in case of volatile market movements since he is not informed about them.

User-oriented risks are strongly related to people risks; particularly the area of communication between staff and computer. In particular, attention should be focused on the controls which are finally executed by staff members. If these controls are ineffective (particularly the interface controls), the processing of data may be affected.

Procedures

A bank's internal procedures and accompanying internal controls are implemented to avoid risks. Nevertheless, they may develop into risks in themselves if:

• a procedure is wrongly designed; or
• a procedure is wrongly executed.

A procedure is wrongly designed if the risks which are caused by a product are not (correctly) controlled. This may happen if these risks are not completely understood by the responsible management. Some risks are not directly evident and are related to implicit products; for example some mortgage loans include so-called embedded options where the customer has the right to fix the interest rate for a certain period during the first year of the loan. If this feature is not noticed, then the interest-rate risk related to this option will not be recorded.

If procedures are not complied with they may be as dangerous as the risks themselves, since they are simply ineffective.

External Risks

The following subcategories can be mentioned for external risks:

• Risks regarding external services and suppliers.
• External criminal activities.
• Disasters.

Risks regarding external services and suppliers have become more and more important in recent years. Outsourcing is a clear trend, which can be both a risk-mitigating measure and a source of risk at the same time. Risks may, for example, originate from not meeting the quality criteria as specified in the service-level agreement. Bankruptcy of the third party is an extreme situation, since for the financial institution an operational risk has become an acute credit risk.

External criminal activities may occur such as bombing and terrorist activities, money laundering and external fraud (especially in the case of payment orders), and damages caused by social unrest among the population. A new element is the damage of web sites of financial institutions, where criminal activity is expressed in the misuse of frames on those sites for own purposes. In some cases the credit card number of the customer is required, and as a result the possibilities of fraud have been magnified.

A final category includes disasters such as flood, hurricanes, earthquakes, power failure and the non-availability of the building. This may be the case after fire, when investigations are still ongoing, or if dangerous materials have been emitted.

Elements of Operational Risk Control

After the classification and identification of risks, the following control elements will now be discussed:

- Risk quantification.
- Risk mitigation and damage control.

Risk Quantification

Even after identification of the risks, quantification is only possible if the amounts of damage and risk probabilities are determined. Operational risks, however, are hard to quantify, since loss histories are mostly not available and some risks cannot easily be displayed in numbers. Although the expected loss may only be estimated if the probabilities of loss are known, the derivation of these probabilities is hardly able to be carried out in practice; a generally-accepted approach is still unavailable. In Chapter 2 the first ideas for a statistical approach will be discussed in more detail.

The expected damages can be a direct loss or an indirect loss. Indirect losses are often of a bigger magnitude: as when the loss of a customer is represented by the present value of all future gains. The level of expected damage is also a benchmark for the implementation of internal and damage controls; the cost of controls should not exceed the expected damage amount. When the expected damage has been calculated, a basis for a risk provision is available. This provision amount may be a part of the solvency requirement regarding operational risk, which is still to be formulated by the regulatory institutions. The Basle Committee will also consider unexpected losses for the determination of the solvency requirement.

Risk Mitigation and Damage Control

Banks should not be passive regarding operational risk; in fact they have various means to prevent or mitigate operational risks, such as:

- internal control measures; and
- internal audit activities.

Internal control measures will be discussed in detail in Chapter 3; segregation of duties, confirmations and dual control can be mentioned as examples.

Internal audit in a bank has the important responsibility of checking whether procedures are followed in practice. Discrepancies are reported and should be addressed by responsible management. Internal auditors could also play an important role in procedure design if they are willing to consult as well.

If an operational risk becomes acute, this does not mean that damage is inevitable. The amount of damage may be reduced by damage control measures, although such controls are mostly of limited development in banks since they are not highly prioritized. If damage occurs, these control measures may protect the bank from high losses. The following elements belong to damage controls:

- damage detection measures;
- a communication plan in the case of damage; and
- an emergency plan in the event of system failures or unavailability of the building.

Damage detection measures can be implemented in a bank's buildings and systems. Some examples are smoke detectors, water detectors in the computer room, an alarm system for secured areas and video control of critical areas. In the system area, capacity management, incident management and problem management may be considered. Such management helps to detect problems and consequent damage may therefore be prevented. Applications may send warning signals, for example if matching between product administration and the general ledger does not lead to the expected results. In this case some data may not be processed, which could cause further damage. If a material accounting entry in the customer's account fails, the customer may dispose of assets wrongly, and the bank is responsible for the resulting damage.

As soon as an error occurs, those persons affected should be informed directly. If the customer knows that a credit accounting entry does not belong to its account, the customer will take note of that information in case of disposal, and consequent damages are therefore prevented. Example 1.5 shows that quick communication between banks can result in limitation of damages.

Damage control measures belong in the toolkit of internal control measures of the risk manager; they will be discussed in detail in Chapter 3.

INTEGRATION OF OPERATIONAL RISK IN BANK MANAGEMENT

The enterprise-wide control of banks is often formulated as integral with performance and risk management,[4] in accordance with one of the oldest

Example 1.5 Stop of payment

The stop-of-payment measure is used to call back ill-processed payment orders which already reside with the receiving bank. For example, the paying bank may perceive too late that the beneficiary on the payment order has been changed (classical fraud case). Paper-based orders are especially vulnerable to this type of fraud, since they go through many hands in the mail process. The changes may be made so professionally that bank employees may be unable to see changes in the document without the help of technical devices.

If the bank uses UV light, it is possible to detect such changes. The bank will then immediately send a stop-of-payment order to the receiving bank. If the transaction is not booked in the beneficiary's account, the receiving bank will normally return the money to the paying bank. The paying bank thus mitigates an operational risk to which it has been exposed.

principles in economics – the scarcity of resources. The enterprise-wide control of banks includes the elements[5] shown in Figure 1.3.

The real bottleneck in banking is the risk absorption possibility. The bank owner's equity determines the amount of risk equivalents, which in itself determines the commercial possibilities of the bank. US-based banks have therefore used the return on allocated capital as a performance measurement criterion for particular business lines for quite some time. The 'risk–reward approach' became common in the banking sector and replaced the old performance measurement criteria such as balance sheet total, net income and the total amount in saving accounts (which was a criterion for the customer's trust in the bank). This paradigm change was the reason for banks to rephrase their management and control approach. In the past banks were managed based on volume growth; today they are managed based on the capital at risk. As a result, the performance of various business lines can be better compared. The bank itself is seen as a portfolio, holding the business lines.

The various business lines of a bank can be valued individually, but complementary effects should be considered as well. The bank's management will review the combination of the portfolio on a regular basis in order to see if it matches with the bank's strategy. It has been observed in the recent past that universal banks have concentrated on particular industries or products. Particular customer segments or product groups were abandoned in order to focus on the future.

16

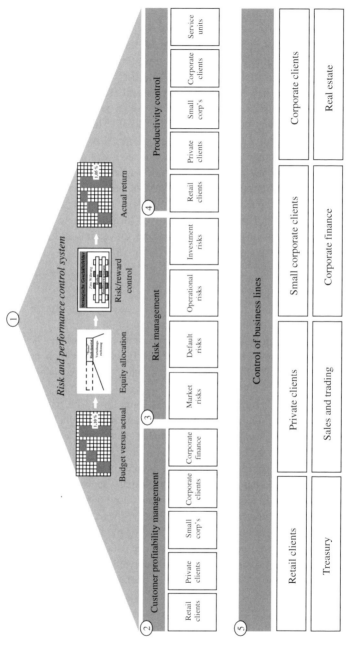

Figure 1.3 The structure of a modern banking control system

Another trend which can be noticed over the last few years is the segmentation of the value-added chain. Many bank activities can be outsourced, like IT services, security settlement and payment services and all supporting activities such as the mailroom. Both trends have influenced the bank's management and control. Outsourcing of parts of the value chain implies various measurement issues which not only deal with the price for these services, but also with their quality. A steady quality control seems to be important.

Recent research publications[6] show that control is still quite financially oriented. The importance of non-financial measurements has been known for quite some time, but they are hardly implemented in practice. Parameters such as customer satisfaction, process quality and staff qualifications are consequently not measured so much as the more easily quantifiable aspects such as a department's cost. This trend will be discontinued in this book, since just those qualitative elements play a determining role for the measurement of operational risk in banks.

The main tasks of a bank control model can be specified as follows:

- Decision support by simulation of various scenarios.
- Measurement of the budget versus the actual situation.
- Explanation of possible management alternatives.

Decision support especially involves the valuation and comparison of the various alternatives. It consists of not only the make-or-buy decisions, but also the budget procedures in banks which are calculated on the basis of different market scenarios. Interest-rate expectations, market liquidity prognoses and creditworthiness assumptions play an important role. These parameters will be combined with transactions- and balance-sheet volumes to determine the expected amounts of interest and fee income. The expected income from trading activities, however, is hard to estimate since the level of the open positions are not known in the future. It could possibly be handled if the position limits are taken as a basis for the calculation of the expected income from trading activities.

The contribution margin per business line can be calculated after including cost and risk cost. This process creates a common base for decision-making upon the future of a business line. The budgeted risk cost will in principle be calculated on the basis of the solvency requirements. Such costs are added to a risk provision, and the changes in the risk provision show the quality of the risk control activities in a bank.

If the models are calculated based on the various scenarios, decision-makers will be able to make the consequences of their decisions transparent.

The second task of a bank control model is the comparison of budgeted versus actual numbers. This comparison can be executed for different time intervals; the limit usage of a trading limit should be compared immediately with the limit itself to check if the transaction concerned is allowed. An online real-time match should be possible in this case. However, most banks are still not that advanced in practice; intra-day limits are often formulated, but limit control is not possible, due particularly to system limitations. The missing control causes an operational risk since higher positions may be taken as allowed, which may cause corresponding losses. Therefore the possibility of being able to measure the actual situation should be considered in the design phase of a banking control model to prevent operational risks.

The budget versus actual comparison should not be limited to the classical performance control. Limit controls for, for example, credit and country risk, but market risk should also be considered. A limit and limit control model for operational risk may be realized in future as well.

The control cycle becomes shorter and shorter. For a few years a monthly report is still sufficient, but, currently, daily reporting is standard. Asset and liability management evolves to a daily task, for which the asset and liability committee only formulates guidelines. In the committee meetings the members only exercise control if the daily management complies with the formulated guidelines. The committee also reviews the guidelines itself regarding current market circumstances. It is to be expected that this trend will continue, and it is therefore questionable whether current system architectures will still comply with the new and constantly moving requirements. Also in this case a latent operational risk exists. If a management information system (MIS) receives the necessary data only after the end-of-day process of the processing systems, the MIS will not be able to control intra-day limits. In the best case, management will be able to prove whether intra-day limits were exceeded after the fact. This control, however, is meaningless for the prevention of market risk.

The third task of a banking control model is the explanation of possible management alternatives, which should be transparent on all management levels. Capacity management in the securities settlement department is a good example. If the transaction volumes increase, the settlement capacity should increase accordingly in order to prevent bottlenecks in the processing flow. It could mean that new staff should be hired and trained on time. Another alternative may be further automation of the processing flow itself; each alternative should be quantified in order to enable a solid decision. Another example is the optimization of an allocated owner's equity on an enterprise level. The following issues can be reviewed: With which counterparties are deals closed? Should derivatives be used to optimize the credit risk? Should syndication of a portfolio or a large engagement be considered? Also in this case alternatives should be recognized and valued by the management information system in order to enable decisions.

The introduction of new products and business lines lies on a strategic level. Sometimes a discussion about the appropriateness of certain functions and products in the current situation is necessary as well. These items should be calculated using the banking control model in order to value each issue.

In the light of operational risk, the performance measurement of processes is seen as critical. Banking processes are highly automated in many cases, and therefore a control system should continually check if the available processing capacity fulfils the needed capacity based on the transaction volume received. Both human and system capacity such as memory, network and external memory should be considered. The control system should warn the processing managers if a bottleneck appears in the process flow. Sometimes the control system may be so 'intelligent' that it may decide on solutions itself.

All these items show that the control of operational risk is an evident task of the banking control model. The most important reasons to consider operational risk explicitly in the banking control model are:

- The influence of operational risk on the allocation of owner's equity over the various business lines.
- The need to control operational risk such as credit risk and market risk.

The allocation of owner's equity is one of the most critical decisions which have to be made by the bank's top management. The management determines where the scarcest resources of the bank will be used. A wrong decision may be accompanied by high opportunity cost and may mean a missed opportunity in another business line at the same time (Figure 1.4). Therefore the allocation of owner's equity is only meaningful if operational risk is considered explicitly. This approach will result in other decisions than simply an implicit consideration of operational risk. In Chapter 2 the quantification of operational risk will be discussed in more detail, here it suffices to say that departments with a relatively high operational risk may become less attractive following an explicit consideration of operational risk. For example the return on a structured product in the treasury or corporate finance department may diminish if the capital allocation for operational risk is taken into account.

Operational risk should not be measured simply to enable a correct allocation of owner's equity; risk mitigation should be the first target, since

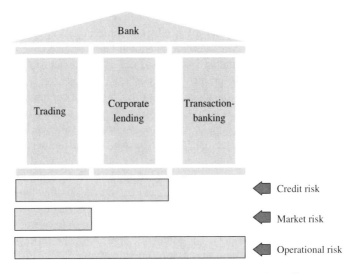

Figure 1.4   Capital allocation to the various business lines

that is one of the main tasks of the bank's management. Therefore unique indicators should be identified for operational risk to enable all management levels to improve on time. Management may sometimes decide that the risk is unavoidable, in which case it may decide to insure the risk. For example, banks are able to insure against fraud caused by both employees and customers.

The need for a clear notification of operational risk in the bank control model has been explained in this chapter; in the coming chapters the concrete implementation in MIS will be discussed.

2 Risk Identification and Quantification

THE AWARENESS PROCESS

Awareness is the most important factor in the control of operational risk. Senior management should not only be familiar with the consequences, but also with the causes of operational risk. Especially for managing board members who do not originate from a more operational part of the bank, it may be hard to identify the risks themselves. In particular, the systems part of operational risk may cause difficulties.

The impression should be avoided that operational risk exists in just the operations area of a bank. Operational risk always exists where people, systems or procedures are working, or where the financial institution is exposed to an external risk. It may therefore be quite hard to identify an area in a bank which is free from any operational risk. In this chapter a more qualitative approach will be discussed: the self-diagnosis and the role of the internal audit department. Current statistical approaches will be discussed afterwards.

SELF-DIAGNOSIS

'Prevention is better than cure', is an old practised rule in the medical world. Self-diagnosis is a good instrument for the prevention of operational risks; it enables managers to check systematically if their departments contain risks which are still unnoticed. In this section the stages of self-diagnosis will be discussed.

Self-diagnosis is, moreover, a means to check if the internal control framework in itself is complete. Internal controls mostly influence the efficiency of operations negatively, and therefore it is quite important to keep procedures as simple as possible. Although business process redesign will not be discussed in this book, it can be a good instrument to detect and improve old and inefficient procedures which are often not, or incompletely, adjusted to new requirements. The final step in the self-diagnosis process can be a periodical review of the efficiency of the set of internal control measures. The results of the self-diagnosis should also be included in the bank's management information.

Self-diagnosis will only be successful if judgement is executed as objectively as possible. The goal of self-diagnosis is to envisage the operational risks as clearly as possible to enable management to minimize found risks in the improvement phase. In the diagnosis phase there are no winners or losers; losers will only exist if the self-diagnosis is not executed seriously.

Information Needed for the Quick-Scan Process

Before a self-diagnosis can be started, a quick scan should be executed. A quick scan enables a priority ranking of various procedures based on the operational risk involved to direct attention to the critical issues immediately. The following information should be available before a quick scan can be started (if this information is lacking, estimates may replace the information):

- An organization chart.
- An IT architecture overview and the corresponding data flows.
- All procedures.
- Transaction volumes.
- An overview of the maximum processing capacity.
- Internal audit reports.
- Overtime reports over the last six months.
- Performance reports (budget versus actual) per department.
- Employee fluctuation reports.
- An overview of customer complaints.
- An open confirmations report.
- An open nostro items report.
- An open suspense accounts items report.
- An overview of system failures.

Organization Chart

The organization chart of a bank shows whether the necessary segregations of duties are implemented. Segregations of duties are normally based on natural contradictions between areas. An authorized decision-maker will never report less cash outflows than he has signed off. The cashier, however, will never report more cash than he has available in the safe. It could be interesting to the cashier to report less than available, since he would then be able to take the money out of the bank's circuit and use it for his own purposes. Since both persons report their activities, a reconciliation between both reports will show that both employees have reported correctly.

The supervisory authorities also have clear requirements regarding the organization structure of a bank. In Vol. 7, 'Basic Principles of Banking Supervision', of the Centre for Central Banking Studies[1] series *Handbooks in Central Banking*, it is pointed out that segregation of duties ('perhaps the oldest and most fundamental control in banking') is required to limit the scope for staff fraud. The segregation of duties between dealing activities and the supporting confirmation and settlement tasks performed in the back office is given as a key example. Most supervisory authorities have formulated such requirements. The German Supervisory Authority[2] even requires that the segregation of duties between trading and back-office/risk-controlling activities is available at the managing board level as well.

If the organization chart of a bank is fragmented, the danger of insufficient bank internal reconciliations exists. In some company cultures it is desired that each staff member is represented in the organization chart, and consequently many tasks which have a logical relationship are decomposed. The bank creates unnecessary interfaces in its organization which need to be reconciled. These reconciliations are not only inefficient, they are also a source of errors if they are executed wrongly or incompletely. A reconciliation of just one item may cause considerable damage: if the account of central bank is reconciled with the general ledger account and two different items are wrongly matched, the bank may believe that a payment which has been charged to the customer's account has been paid to the beneficiary's bank. This may not be the case, and damage has already been caused. The bank is liable for the delay interest charges and probably for other damages suffered by its customer as well.

A matrix organization may lead to confusion regarding responsibilities. In many cases regional, functional and product responsibilities exist. Each bank which chooses a matrix organization is confronted with the problem of defining areas of responsibility. If the responsibility areas are not clearly defined, one responsible staff member may think that the control tasks are executed by the other responsible manager. If all responsible managers think in this way, the consequence will be that nobody is really in control. In Figure 2.1 an organization chart is shown which explains the problem of a matrix organization.

IT Architecture Overview and the Corresponding Data Flows

In recent years banks have become more and more dependent on their IT systems, and it would be hard to imagine today's common transaction volumes without any technical support. Banks have especially automated their volume-intensive business. As a result, 'island solutions' have been

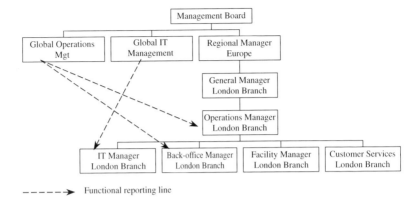

Figure 2.1   Matrix organization

created which can hardly communicate with each other. Another issue is the different life-cycles of banking products. A derivative, for example, has a much shorter life-cycle than a normal term loan; a derivative may be trendy today, but can be obsolete tomorrow. This may be a consequence of the desired flexibility in the derivatives area.

Such differences make an integral IT solution almost impossible. If all products and processes are to be part of an integral IT solution, a big problem may occur with the release cycle of the software. Derivatives processing may, for example, need monthly releases, instead of term-loan processing which may only need a new release after three years. Moreover, a complete coverage of all banking products makes the system so complex that an overview may be lost. A lost overview becomes clear if data or information are not reconcilable anymore and nobody knows why a difference occurred.

Different systems, however, imply many interfaces. Their quality is not always guaranteed and therefore the danger of non-integer data exists. Both the design of the interface itself which depends highly on the right data definition, and the data import process which may not be error-free due to technical issues, determine the quality of data. Each interface, however, needs its own reconciliation process. That this issue may have a big impact – even in a smaller bank – is shown in Figure 2.2.

As already mentioned, each interface needs its own reconciliation, which may vary for each interface. In the case of Reuters data, which is be used for the valuation of the trading portfolio, the most important check is the date check. Otherwise the trading portfolio would be valued with outdated rates. Furthermore, a check with yesterday's data may be a reasonable

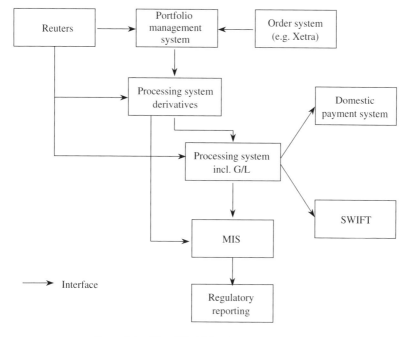

Figure 2.2   Simplified IT architecture of a bank

requirement since even Reuters sometimes delivers false data. Big rela-
tional differences may be caused by wrong data, and so they should be
checked in detail.

The interface between the processing system and the domestic payments
system should especially ensure that all payment orders from the processing system are correctly received and processed. If payment orders do not
come through, the bank will be confronted with interest payments. If the
customer suffers other damages as well due to late payment, the bank may
be charged with these amounts as well.

A special issue is the quality of the hardware and software used by the
bank. If old processing systems are used, there may be limited flexibility.
Old hardware may cause maintenance problems since certain parts may no
longer be available. If the bank uses its own developed software, it often
happens after some time that no single programmer knows the exact relationships of all program modules any more. If documentation is available,
its quality is often so poor that it hinders rather than helps. This problem
was such that many already-retired programmers were called back to their

jobs to deal with the year 2000 problems: the COBOL knowledge of current staff was inadequate to solve the problem without help.

Moreover, many banks do not know why certain data flows exist. Nevertheless, nobody wants to take the responsibility to stop or change these data flows, since nobody can estimate what the consequences will be. Therefore much energy is sacrificed to activities which are of no advantage to the bank. The IT architecture and data flows alone explain a good part of the operational risk status of a bank. If both areas are not documented properly, it is often a clear identification that a potential operational risk exists.

All Procedures

Procedures are the central focus for the diagnosis of operational risk. However, it is impossible to check all banking procedures in detail in the quick-scan phase, so that a quick scan should be limited to the important procedures. One of these describes how procedures are designed and authorized in the bank, and the following points should be considered:

- Are all relevant features of the products involved defined and considered in the design of the procedure?
- Are all risks involved with both the products and the procedure itself sufficiently documented, and is it known which risk-mitigating measures have to be implemented?
- Are the functions used in the procedure really needed?
- Is each procedure of all involved responsible staff members approved and signed?
- Is the procedure accepted by the internal audit department and has the procedure been signed off for acceptance?
- Are all new and changed procedures documented in an orderly manner and are all involved employees informed in time?

Besides a check on the procedure for design, a check on a small sample of existing procedures should be executed. It is advised to consider the following:

- Reconciliation of suspense accounts.
- Reconciliation of nostro accounts.
- A procedure regarding security trading.
- A procedure regarding payment services.
- A procedure regarding the collection of management information.

The first two of these can identify if the bank is control-oriented. The reconciliation of suspense and nostro accounts is important to control if the entire settlement process is functioning properly. Older open items may be a warning signal for a possible operational risk; if employees do not pay enough attention to the open items they may cause big losses to the bank. It is well-known in the banking sector that fraud is mostly conducted in relation to suspense accounts.

Procedures in the securities trading and payment services area normally give a good indication of the quality of other procedures in the bank, since they describe one of the most sensible areas in the bank. Settlements errors do not just damage the bank financially, they may also disturb the trust relationship between the customer and the bank.

The procedure for management information collection identifies the knowledge of the MIS department about the data in the various systems. If this knowledge is only partly available, then management information may be incomplete or false and may lead to unfortunate decisions.

Transaction Volumes

Transaction volumes and their volatility tell something about the operational risk, if the available processing capacity is considered as well. It is quite logical to process as close as possible to the capacity limits for economic reasons, but this approach is a source of disturbances at the same time. Problems may occur in both the human resources and systems area. It is not only the full usage of the available capacity which may lead to problems. Big changes in processing volume may cause operational risks as well, since employees have to adjust to a changing situation. The number of errors caused by stress may also increase.

Changes in the volume of transactions to be processed do not cause problems to employees only: systems may also not function error-free any more if volumes increase too rapidly. This problem has become real in the on-line banking environment. After the successful introduction of the internet, banks started to introduce on-line banking as well. The ability to manage both payments and securities was interesting for many people who wished to invest money in securities or even to trade professionally. Day trading started, since information on market prices and events is available on the internet with only small time delays (real-time information as such is still a myth!). Banks had to create new systems to be able to offer these internet services, but the processing systems are still the same good old ones. Since the banking world is quite conservative, the hard-core processing systems are quite old, and no decision-maker likes to change because of the uncertainty of a successful new implementation. These systems have been maintained over years, and it is quite hard to specify all the small changes that have happened. If a new system were to be implemented, it is quite sure that some of these small but vital changes may be overlooked. Although this situation is a big operational risk in itself, banks believe that the risk of renewal may be larger.

One of the key issues, of course, has been the connection between the new internet world and the old processing machines. The old processing machines were accustomed to manual data entry and verification. Therefore their processing capacity did not need to be very high since the data entry itself took time. Moreover, processing capacity (especially internal memory) was quite scarce when the processing applications were built, and application designers tried to save as much internal memory as possible. The new internet world, however, brought some significant changes for the old processing systems. Instead of manual entry, data entry was executed by interfaces. The internet server collects the transactions which are delivered on-line and forwards these to the processing systems. The prudence of the past in saving internal memory has become a bottleneck in this new situation. The consequences are quite severe: since the so-called 'buffers' may overflow, transactions may be lost without any notice. This is a real acute operational risk.

Direct banks have become popular in Germany in the last few years, but the stream of new customers could not be processed in an orderly manner. Also, transaction processing was seriously delayed. Due to increased transparency – through the internet – customers were able to see if transactions were not forwarded to the exchange directly. In spring 2000 even the supervisory authority publicly said that this situation was unacceptable and required the managing boards of the direct banks to improve it quickly. It is clear that the flow of transaction orders increases if markets become more volatile, and if transactions are processed too late, rates may decrease and the customer will claim the difference to the rate at the moment of order with the bank. Both issues, the transaction capacity usage and the transaction volume development should be examined not only in a quick scan; at least the managers responsible for settlement activities should be regularly informed about the transaction capacity usage and the transaction volume development. If this is currently not the case, the bank should use the opportunity to integrate this information into the management information.

Overview of the Maximum Processing Capacity

Although this information is more static, it still forms a limitation for all the bank's activities. If banks are not aware of the maximum processing capacity, planning errors may occur. The determination of this capacity, however, is not so easy. A systems supplier will hardly be able to indicate how many transactions per cycle can be processed, since the maximum processing capacity is determined by the process as a whole.

The following items (not limited) may have considerable impact on the processing capacity:

- On-line interfaces to other systems (e.g. for limit checks).
- On-line calculations to determine limit usage (especially in the case of more complex statistical calculations).
- The quality of the transaction information itself.
- The processing knowledge of the employees involved.

The determination of the maximum processing capacity may only be successful by testing in the bank's specific situation. The determination is more valuable if a staircase cost effect is to be expected. Highly-automated processes such as the mass transaction processing area are vulnerable regarding the fixed-cost problem. Planning without this information may even cause actual losses instead of expected gains.

Internal Audit Reports

The internal audit departments of banks have mostly adapted to their new environment in the last few years. In the past the audit function was directed towards compliance with law and regulations. In some cases the internal audit activities were to a large extent supportive to the external auditor in the case of financial audit. Today the internal audit plans are based on a sound risk analysis as well. Internal auditors focus more on the risky areas in the bank to optimize the limited audit time available. Moreover, many internal audit departments have moved to operational audit; the relevance of the operational audit function for operational risk analysis is discussed later in this chapter.

The internal audit reports can be helpful in discovering which processes are most risky. The diagnosis phase should start with the procedures in which the most deficits were found during audits. The audit judgement of the internal auditor can also be the basis for the comparison of risks. If, for example, many negative audit findings are found regarding the ordering procedure in the facility department, the risk concerning these audit findings may be far lower than the risk of an inappropriate segregation of duties in the procedures of the payment department.

The internal audit reports also show how procedures are functioning. Even if a procedure is well-designed and implemented, it may still occur that staff do not act in compliance with the procedure. This problem can only be systematically discovered in a quick scan if the internal audit department consequently audits and reports the results in their reports.

A check on the knowledge of the internal auditors should be included in the quick scan as well. Focus should be directed especially towards products and procedures in the investment banking area. New products steadily come to the market, which have all their own risk profile; if the internal auditor is not able to determine the risk profile of each product, he will not be able to discover the risks involved during his audit. It is even possible that blank fields exist in the bank since risks may not be weighted correctly in the audit plans and therefore audits may not be conducted in the right time intervals. A quick identification of the current knowledge in the internal audit department is important for the internal auditors.

Overtime Report over the Last Six Months

It has already been pointed out in Chapter 1 that employees are not able to work to the same high level continuously. In some areas pauses should regularly be built in, in order to maintain the high concentration levels needed. Continuous overtime may indicate the following problems:

• The department is not in control.
• Activities are not well-proportioned to the staff available.
• Some colleagues like to create overtime for their own reasons.

The department is not in control if just some employees take overtime and other staff members go home at five. In such cases the proportioning of activities should be redesigned to optimize the capacity usage and to increase employees' satisfaction.

Ill-designed procedures may sometimes be the cause of overtime as well. For example, if procedures are only partly adapted to a new system implementation one should not be amazed if this leads to more overtime. Sometimes activities have to be duplicated or data entry is only possible under sub-optimal conditions. Sometimes overtime may be caused by small issues like different routing on forms and screens. Such differences not only cause stress to the employees, since data entry becomes slower, but they may also result in errors since employees may still fall back to the old data-entry procedures.

Another possibility is that activities have to be conducted by less staff. Especially in areas where the labour market is small may this situation exist. At this moment it appears to be hard to recruit well-experienced staff in the IT and securities settlement area. This situation may be dissatisfying for staff in these areas as well, since they have to take structural overtime,

Example 2.1 The forgotten EUREX update

The bank is a EUREX member and has experienced a strong increase in the futures transaction area in the last few months. The bank is cost-sensitive and therefore the IT department has remained small; only two system administrators are familiar with the EUREX application. Due to longer trading times the bank has to recruit additional staff at an unfortunate moment, since all banks are more or less in the same situation. Both system administrators take structural overtime and both are quite busy. One receives a letter from EUREX which announces a new update, which has to be implemented in his vacation. He archives the letter in the false file. As his vacation comes closer, the system administrator is happy to see his little daughter awake and he does not remember the letter about the EUREX update, so his colleague is not informed about it.

At the implementation day, the second system administrator goes home early because of the beautiful weather. The day afterwards he comes in the bank not imagining what has happened, but his phone is already ringing. It is the futures trader. The EUREX connection is not available, just at the exercise date on which the trader normally executes many transactions. The system administrator immediately makes some routine checks but he is not able to find the cause of the lost connection: the real cause lies in his colleague's file, and in the fact that the bank was not able to recruit extra staff in order to mitigate the pressure on both system administrators.

As time runs, the losses increase.

which may result in errors. Such problems may be judged critical if it affects the system administrators, since they may be excellent problem multipliers. See Example 2.1.

Some employees, however, like to make overtime; but if an employee makes much overtime and takes no vacation, it should be checked in more detail during the quick scan whether this person is a workaholic or is conducting fraud.

Performance Reports (Budget versus Actual) per Department

Performance reports are one of the basic control instruments in a bank. The information should not only contain the variances between budgeted versus actual values for a profit- or cost-centre, but should also represent

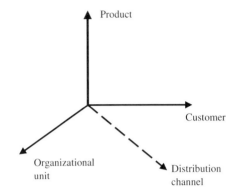

Figure 2.3   Dimensions of performance measurement

the values per customer and product. At the end, the staff responsible for relationship management and product management should be able to check their performance as well. Performance control has four dimensions as shown in Figure 2.3.

The performance reports should not be limited to a quantitative analysis of the variances. Large variances could identify an implementation problem in the bank, but they may be a result of bad planning as well. The last point should also be reflected in the quick scan since this may identify an under-developed control awareness in the bank. It is important to check during the quick scan if the analysis of the variances is clearly documented. The responsible staff members should be able to make plausible statements to the variances and be able to describe the measures taken to improve the actual current situation. The controller of the bank should only accept these action plans if the planned measures are reasonable. The controller also controls if the measures are implemented on time and if they result in the desired effect. If the procedure is designed and implemented as described here, it can be assumed in the quick-scan process that the control procedures and the control environment in the bank are functioning.

Employee Fluctuation Report

The fluctuation of employees is mostly highest in the areas where recruitment of new staff is most difficult. The positions can mostly only be occupied by specialists. The IT department in most banks is a clear example of this problem; the market for IT specialists remains stressed even after the millennium change, since many projects were delayed to after

January 2000 and they still remain to be implemented. A high employees' fluctuation means:

- A loss of know-how in the organization.
- Many new employees have to be introduced to their jobs and they will all make some start-up errors.
- The employees' satisfaction may be low.

If a bank does not have a functioning knowledge-management system, the bank will lose knowledge all the time when employees resign. Mostly employees do not document exactly which tasks have to be fulfilled in their jobs. As long as everything functions fine, this deficit is only latent. If something special like a system failure or late data delivery happens, the new employees probably do not know how to mitigate these problems. Experienced staff members, however, know which mitigating measures have to be taken based on their know-how collected over many years.

Experienced colleagues are not able to take care of all new staff members individually if many vacancies have to be filled; therefore more errors occur than necessary. The new employees probably have to look for a solution themselves, which will be sub-optimal in most cases and therefore not error-free. A quick introduction to the job may cause problems in the long run which might not have happened had the fluctuation rate not been so high.

Sometimes the bank is not able to fill vacancies despite all efforts. In this case employees have to take structural overtime which may lead to errors, dissatisfaction and finally to their resignation.

Overview of Customer Complaints

The analysis of customer complaints may identify structural problems. Information from such complaints should contain the error type and the procedure in which the error has occurred, and the analysis of this information may identify the cause of the errors. One of the causes, for example, may be an ill-designed procedure. In this case a structural error has been found which can be excluded and result in a complete disappearance of the mentioned error. But incidental errors also exist. Their causes can hardly be systematically recorded and therefore improvement of these errors will not have such a great effect as in the case of structural errors.

During the quick scan, not only the type and frequency of errors but also their improvement should be analysed. Some banks have a '24-hours policy' which means that errors should be improved completely satisfactorily in one day. If a solution cannot be arranged on time, the customer has to be informed about the status of the measures taken. Such customer complaint systems have the feature that unsolved complaints older than one day are automatically reported to the department head. It is quite interesting to check during the quick scan what happens with such complaints, since a customer complaint is not just an identification of an operational risk but may also be the start of a reputation loss. If the error is serious or more small errors come together, the trust relationship with the customer may be disturbed, which may result in termination of the relationship.

The number of errors and, more particularly, the solution of the errors are an identification of the control awareness of the organization. The way problems are solved needs attention during the quick scan.

Open Confirmations Report

Confirmations are important in the settlement of investment banking products. Normally the bank receives a confirmation from its counterparty to confirm that the transaction was closed with the mentioned conditions. The bank also sends such a confirmation. The counterparty signs the confirmations for agreement if the details are correct (normally according to their proxy the document is signed off by two employees) and sends them back. Confirmations are not used between counterparties in all cases, however. In the case of money-market trades confirmations are normally not used. If the bank takes money, the counterparty normally transfers the money within two days; the payment itself is the best confirmation the bank can receive.

Derivatives, however, have other cash-flow features, and confirmations play an important role in this area. The deal date and the first settlement date may vary more than six months. For example if a swap transaction is closed (see Figure 2.4) with the following features:

- The bank pays the counterparty a fixed rate over the nominal amount with an interest period of five years.
- The bank receives a variable rate over the nominal amount related to the EURIBOR (Euro Interbank Offered Rate) and a spread with an interest period of six months.

If the bank does not receive confirmation from its counterparty, the bank will be confronted with a failing cash inflow after six months. The trader may have reversed the transaction with the counterparty, but he forgot to reverse the transaction in the front-office system. During this six months the bank would include this non-existing transaction in all risk reports. If the transaction contains a huge amount, the damage to the bank may be considerable if market interest rates have been increased over time. Moreover,

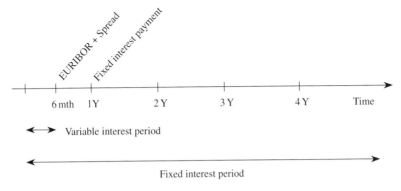

Figure 2.4 Cash-flow pattern of an interest-rate swap

the bank's regulatory reporting was wrong since it includes a non-existing swap. This may result in a reputation risk as well.

This risk may be prevented by a well-defined procedure regarding the matching of confirmations. If confirmations remain open after a week, the counterparty should be called to clarify if it received the confirmation. The counterparty may need further clarifications which may be given during the telephone call. The department head should review each transaction which has an open confirmation older than one week. If the bank does not receive a signed confirmation after the second request, the department head himself should contact the counterparty. If this contact is also unsuccessful, the transaction should be reported to senior management and the internal audit department. Normally the internal auditor contacts his colleague at the counterparty to clarify the situation. Senior management should decide to request the internal audit department to check the transaction in detail (it could be a fraud case) and the management may forbid any new transactions with the counterparty until further notice.

Many open confirmations which have an unclear status are a sign of a non-control-minded organization. In case of a quick scan, the risks involved should be made clear.

Open Nostro Items Report

The nostro accounts are used for the settlement of foreign payments. Banks look for correspondent banks abroad and open nostro accounts with those banks. If the bank has to settle a payment to a beneficiary in the country of the correspondent bank, the correspondent bank is ordered to pay the amount to (the bank of) the beneficiary and to charge the nostro account of the ordering bank. In order to fund that payment, the ordering bank will take money out of the market (by trading a deposit in foreign currency or a fx-spot transaction) with a settlement instruction 'nostro account with the correspondent bank'.

Open nostro items may have different causes, for example:

- The correspondent bank did not execute the payment order;
- The correspondent bank did not receive an order; or
- Due to an accounting error a suspense account has the contrary open items as well.

In all mentioned cases the bank will be confronted with a loss, which may only be partly forwarded to the loss-causing party. In all situations the bank will try to minimize the losses for the bank's customer.

Open nostro items cost money. Credit balances do not normally bear any interest, but debit balances, however, are charged with high interest rates. Large banks may suffer interest losses amounting to millions of pounds. Also, losses are not limited to interest losses: open items may be caused by fraud as well and these issues should be detected as early as possible. A large number of open nostro items – especially older ones – show that the organization does not have the nostro-linked processes under control.

Open Suspense Accounts Items Report

The balances of suspense accounts have to be clearly explicable at all times. Suspense accounts are used in praxis to facilitate reconciliations and to record asynchrony transactions; if the bank trades securities today, the cash inflow and the delivery of securities will be in two days. Therefore the amount is booked in a suspense account. Sometimes accounting entries come in, but the target account is unclear (for example a payment comes in, but the account number does not exist). The items are booked in a suspense account to prevent disruption to the normal processing flow. Moreover, the constant monitoring of these accounts will ensure quick detection and hope-fully a quick solution. As soon as the target of the accounting entry is clear, the suspense account will be cleared. The monitoring process should ensure that these types of suspense accounts are clean at the end of each day.

Suspense accounts should always be assigned to a responsible staff member who is responsible for the regular reconciliation of the account and the clar-ification of the open items. If nobody is responsible, the bank is exposed to an operational risk since anybody may book into the suspense account but the open items are not clarified. Such a situation may be an open invitation for fraud. During the quick scan is should be checked if all suspense accounts are assigned to responsible staff members, without any exception.

The number of suspense accounts already tells us something about the organization of a bank. Principally, as many suspense accounts should be opened as necessary but as few as possible. They should be embedded in processes and not just be opened per department. In particular, it should be checked whether open items in suspense accounts are 'refreshed' by transferring them from the original suspense account to another suspense account. Such accounting entries are an effective means to hide fraud. Especially accounts with many accounting entries with the same amount need attention during the quick scan. In cases of fraud, the employee may take out one of the transactions and use the money for personal purposes; the pattern of such fraud is shown in Example 2.2.

Many open items often indicate a capacity problem in the settlement organization of the bank; departments are not able to clarify the open items on time. Such a situation is often a good base for fraudulent transactions.

Overview of System Failures

System failures also have a time dimension as well as a damage dimension. The time dimension becomes more visible in the case of cut-off times, for

---

Example 2.2 Fraud and suspense accounts

Fixed fees for current accounts are booked in a suspense account on a monthly basis; afterwards fees are allocated to the profit centres. The employee who is responsible for this account has been preparing the accounting entries for years. The employee discovers by accident how the 'past due' procedure functions; after one month clients are requested to pay the fees. The employee therefore books one amount not in the profit centre account, but in the current account of his cousin in order to cover the fraudulent transaction.

Before a month passes the employee books a 'fresh' received fee in the profit centre account, he simply acts as if this amount is the transaction which he paid to the current account of his cousin. The responsible staff member for the profit centre is happy, and does not need to send out a reminder letter.

The employee may repeat this process each month and he is able to invest the money and to benefit from the interest. This type of fraud will only be discovered if the employee is on vacation or ill, and therefore unable to move a transaction to the profit centre on time.

example when payment orders have to be delivered to the clearing house before a certain time to guarantee same-day processing. It may be clear that a system failure at 7 a.m. has different consequences to the same system failure just 15 minutes before cut-off time. The damage is far bigger in the last case since customer payment orders will not be processed in time. Moreover, the bank is exposed to a reputation loss as well, since the clearing process does not become final. All clearing members have to wait longer before the final payments can be processed in their systems. In the worst case the bank has to execute lump-sum payments to banks to avoid high interest penalties. Such payments should more or less compensate the amount which normally should have been paid.

System failures often cause a great deal of manual activities. If for example interfaces between systems do not function, it may be necessary to execute double data entry. Although it depends on the number of transactions if double data entry is possible, such manual processing is always accompanied by much stress. Cut-off times may especially increase pressure. It is clear that stress in this case may also be the cause of new errors.

The consequences of a system failure should be recognized as well. It is hard to estimate which other systems and procedures are affected by the system failure, but the following problems may occur:

- The data delivery to other systems is not executed.
- The data import was not executed.
- The system performed calculations based on an incomplete data set.
- The system created reports based on an incomplete data set.

System administrators need an exact procedure to determine if all data flows are complete. If this is not the case, data has to be delivered again. This process can often not be started automatically, which implies the next risk: that abusively a second processing of the same data may be executed. It is therefore advisable to introduce a control system to ensure complete and correct data import and export between systems. This system then reports to the system administrator if data flows were not generated correctly. The control concerning complete data is not simple, but a comparison of file sizes at the source system and the receiving system may prevent much damage.

Whether the system calculated with a complete data set is not easy to prove. The necessary reconciliation which is needed to demonstrate a complete data set can often not be executed automatically. Incomplete calculations and reports may cause wrong decisions and consequent losses. If the frequency of system failures is high, the quality of the control procedure regarding system availability should be checked during the quick scan. A good control procedure should prevent the risks described in this section.

Results of the Quick Scan

The results of a quick scan should enable a bank's senior management to make a risk-weighted priority of the necessary diagnostic activities. Senior management is responsible for the realization of the formulated targets without exposing the bank to too much risk. Regarding credit risk, the methodological and quantitative approaches have reached a stage which allows a first practical usage. The (internal) rating approach will then be implemented.

Market risk can be represented properly, and in the meantime the methods of risk control are common knowledge in the bank at all management levels. Operational risk, however, has a different nature, since the risk has more dimensions. Credit risk and market risk can be associated with certain activities in the bank; operational risk cannot be localized that easily. Normally, operational risk does not cause existence-threatening losses on a daily basis. On the contrary, the losses caused by operational risk are mostly moderate.

The risk features may hinder management in finding the right approach to operational risk. The field of operational risk is so wide that priorities have to be set. Therefore a quick scan report should help management to rank the processes for which a diagnosis phase is needed. If, for example, the employees' fluctuation is quite high, the cause of this fluctuation should be found. The first question is whether management itself is aware of the problem and has already started to analyse it. There is always a big difference between 'knowing things' and 'thinking we know things'. Sometimes management does not want to consider reality, since the real causes of the problem may be unpleasant to face. In that case management should become aware of its exposure to risk by ignoring reality.

The question remains, which processes have to be investigated. Procedures in the human resources area should definitely be considered. The first question is: How is staff recruited? Is the ability of candidates to cooperate in the existing team checked by the assessors? Has the bank a tutor system to help new colleagues find their way in the organization? Is permanent education part of the human resources services in the bank, or have employees to take care of themselves? Are employees' ideas considered or has the bank just a top-down culture? If appraisals of employees are planned, can employees also articulate their view or is the appraisal limited to a performance review of the employee only? If management receives signals via third employees, are these signals considered seriously even if these staff members are not able to mention the names of colleagues involved? If staff have resigned, are exit interviews held? Exit interviews in particular show management the weak spots in their organization and in their management style. However, exit interviews are often avoided by managers since they fear that the discussion may reveal some unfortunate issues. Each avoided exit interview is a missed chance to learn something about the organization.

All these questions may be asked as a result of the quick scan. The quick scan itself does not give the answers, but it enables management to ask the right questions. The real answers should be found in the diagnosis phase. Based on the quick scan a first overview of the risk intensity of the various procedures exists. The procedure with the highest risk should be investigated first under consideration of the expected amount of damages.

Self-Diagnosis Steps

Self-diagnosis can be started after the risk-based priority setting of all procedures concerned. Some parts of the self-diagnosis, however, may be assessed generally. The structure is shown in Figure 2.5. In the case of human resources, procedures such as recruitment, appraisal and the general conditions could be the subject of investigation. 'Management' is very important in this area, for example if managers require a certain behaviour they should conduct activities in compliance with their own rules; and the quality of this area depends upon the credibility of the behaviour of senior management.

For both areas, human resources and management questions are formulated and included in Appendix 1. These questions are a basic framework;

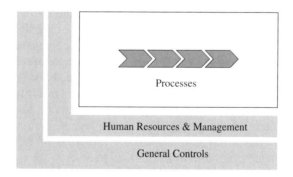

Figure 2.5   General and specific processes

it may happen that some other areas may be investigated in addition due to the bank's specific situation and the question base should be enlarged accordingly.

Another area which can be investigated in general is the design and effectiveness of the general controls regarding IT systems. General controls should ensure a reliable and error-free functioning of the applications. In most banking systems (= applications) it is not possible that an employee is able to verify transactions which are entered by himself, since this would mean a breach of the segregation of duties or dual control. Therefore the data entry and verification function are separated in different functions. If the login procedure, however, is not effective, the employee may be able to verify his own transactions by using a user-id of a colleague. If this is the case for the data entry of payment orders, fraud is made quite easy and errors may be 'pre-programmed'. The same is true for the other general controls like change management and capacity management. Some questions regarding general controls are also included in Appendix 1.

The diagnosis of specific procedures cannot be arranged by just a questionnaire. The following general questions may help to determine if risks are included in the investigated procedure:

- Are the products which are processed in this procedure exactly analysed and are the requirements originating from the product features documented?
- Does the procedure fit the organization and the systems involved?
- Are the internal control measures documented in the procedure and are they integrated at the right points according to the identified risks?

The procedures in a bank should be determined by the product features of the products involved. It can be payment flows per product or the risks involved (like interest-rate risks, gamma effects and so forth). It cannot be generally said which features or risks should be paid attention to. Moreover, the same transactions may be treated differently in different banks. Culture and organization size are, for example, influence factors to the way procedures are organized.

Information deficiencies regarding products may be more easily detected if a controller or internal auditor is consulted. The product features should be described by the departments involved. The risks concerning a product can be both implicit or explicit. The first category is harder to detect. For example, market risks may exist in the credit portfolio which are not immediately visible. If the owner of a house has the right to fix the interest rate for his mortgage loan in the first year, the bank has implicitly written an option which might not be detected during the design of the procedure for risk management.

The fit between procedures, systems and the organization is an important theme. It may seem easy to copy a so-called 'best-practice approach' to the organization, but if these best-practice approaches are based on another organization size or another IT system, the implementation of such procedures may simply introduce new operational risks to the bank instead of avoiding them.

The size of the organization determines the level and the possibilities of segregation of duties. In larger organizations, segregation of duties already exists based on the allocation of activities of staff members and departments. However, in a smaller organization some functions, which should ideally be segregated, need to be combined. Such combination of functions needs to be well-considered since the operational risk, which increases, should be kept as small as possible.

The usage of internal controls depends on the systems used. If an application has been written in Excel, dual control cannot be implemented since each user is able to change values and formulas without any journaling of activities. Data entry and verification cannot be technically separated. Change management is also excluded, since each user can change formulas without testing. If applications are developed for system environments in which general controls cannot be implemented effectively, it is not possible to rely on the application controls. Users are able to pass the application controls if general controls fail. If the risks involved are known, internal controls should be implemented at the right point in the procedures. An internal control measure which is in itself right but implemented at the wrong point, is just as ineffective as a failing internal control measure. This point should be thoroughly investigated during the self-diagnosis.

The internal control measures – the toolkit for operational risk management – will be discussed in Chapter 3.

Use of the Questionnaire

The questionnaire covers four themes, all related to operational risk:

- Human resources
- Management
- Systems
- Processes

The questions sometimes have a general nature, although the systems questions always refer to the systems which are involved in the investigated process. For example the payment system is irrelevant if the financial information process for the completion of regulatory reporting is tested.

The questionnaire is definitely not limited in such a way that the complete risk profile for each financial institution can be disclosed. The questionnaire, however, may help to achieve an effective estimation of operational risk in these general processes. If questions are added for certain areas, the diagnosis will be improved. The questions are formulated positively, which means that a positive answer should be categorized under 'good' or 'very good'. For each question group an average quality ranking is calculated to enable senior management to receive a quick overview of the risks involved. This method is sufficient for the awareness phase. All questions will definitely not have the same impact on the operational risk profile of the bank: one question which is answered with 'satisfying' may include a larger exposure to operational risk than an answer 'poor'. Therefore the questions which are answered with 'satisfying' and 'poor' should be analysed in detail in a second round. The comments, which are also included in the questionnaire, may support further analysis.

It is advisable to look for questionnaires in other departments. The internal audit function may also have questionnaires to prepare their audits, which may contain relevant information for operational risk. If all results of the questionnaires are available and the information collected in the quick-scan phase are analysed as well, first conclusions can be drawn. It is reasonable to discuss the results in management meetings to achieve a common improvement action plan. The toolkit discussed in Chapter 3 may be helpful in this phase.

THE INTERNAL AUDIT DEPARTMENT'S ROLE

In the last decade operational audit became a theme for most internal audit departments in financial institutions. Until then, internal audit departments were highly involved in the financial audit, which concentrates on the financial statement of the financial institution. Internal auditors are not allowed to certify the financial statement of the financial institution, but the external auditors rely on the audit findings of the internal audit department if possible. The external auditor's task is made easier if he is able to rely on the financial institution's internal control system. If the external auditor is not able to rely on the internal control system, he needs to perform many verification activities to allow an own-judgement about the quality of the presented information. It is clear that this approach is cost-intensive for the bank.

In this section the operational audit function will be described in order to conclude the value of the operational audit results for the diagnosis of operational risk.

Operational Audit

An operational audit should reassure management that the financial institution's procedures are well-designed and adhered to. Operational audit is therefore seen as a management tool. Operational audit was introduced in the Anglo-Saxon world in the 1990s during the introduction of the integral management concept. Central support departments were reduced or declined, and their functions were moved to a non-central level. Each business line became independently responsible, for example human resources and accounting and control.

The reduction of central functions implied a loss of internal control measures, however, and this internal control gap was closed by the operational audit function. Operational audit follows the management-cycle, as illustrated in Figure 2.6.[3]

In Driessen *et al.* (1993) *Operational Auditing: een managementkundige benadering*, operational audit is clearly seen as a management tool. The operational audit function is responsible for auditing the consistency among the financial institution's strategy, the organization and the execution of the activities required. If discrepancies are found, the operational audit function will also propose improvement actions. The new organization structure will allow the financial institution to react faster and more flexibly to customer

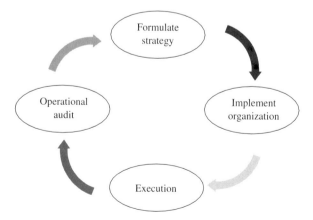

Figure 2.6 The operational audit process

requirements, since all affected functions are located on the decentral level. Short communication channels are therefore guaranteed.

The Value of Operational Audit Reports for Diagnostic Purposes

If the operational audit function in a financial institution exists, the audit findings can be supportive to the diagnosis of operational risks. The findings may reveal:

- If a mismatch exists between the financial institution's strategy and its organization.
- If a mismatch exists between the organization structure including the processes and the requirements based on the current situation.
- If processes and internal controls are efficiently and effectively implemented.

The independence of the operational auditor is seen as an advantage. The operational auditor is not interested in another representation of reality as it really exists.[4] A self-diagnosis, however, may be not so exact, since the assessor may – unaware – overlook a weakness in the organization since he is accustomed to the situation and he assumes the weakness as given.

Operational audit is therefore advisable as a complement to self-diagnosis. Such an operational audit should not necessarily be executed by auditors, but rather by colleagues or consultants with specific expertise. A valuable audit is only possible if sufficient knowledge regarding products, systems and processes is available to the operational auditors. Basic knowledge available to all auditors is mostly insufficient for this kind of audit. In France, all senior managers have to work in the audit department before they are allowed to be a senior manager. The awareness of the importance of internal controls is evident with these managers. The execution of a diagnosis may also be a good opportunity for managers in other countries to learn the skills regarding operational risks and the implementation of an appropriate internal control system.

QUANTIFICATION OF OPERATIONAL RISK

Before the quantification of operational risk is discussed, the target of the results of quantification is explained. In Chapter 1 (p. 14 ff) the important role of the bank's regulatory capital, its scarcest resource was discussed. The regulatory bodies require regulatory capital to mitigate the expected and unexpected risks the bank is exposed to such as credit risks, market risks and operational risks.

It is clear that the bank also needs to manage the allocation of its scarcest resource carefully to achieve its results; the bank's management has to decide on the allocation of capital to the different business lines and products. In particular, if the regulatory capital required by the business lines in their business plans exceeds the available amount of regulatory capital, the bank's management is forced to make choices. It is obvious that the bank's management will optimize their decisions based on the expected return of the products in comparison to the risks involved.

It should be noticed that the regulatory capital is not the same variable as the bank's economic capital. Since the regulatory capital amount is based on the calculation formulas as required by the regulatory authorities, the fit to the risks the bank is really exposed to is sub-optimal. The regulatory authority has to create a common level playing field for all banks, and they therefore need to use simplifications of reality. Simplifications are even made regarding the calculation of market risk, although internal models are allowed to calculate the solvency requirement regarding such risk. The same is true for the old calculation method for the solvency requirement regarding credit risk: no differentiation was made regarding the creditability of the bank's customers. An unsecured credit to the baker in a small village was charged with the same capital amount as an unsecured credit to an AA-rated company. The Basle Committee will address this issue in the new capital accord.

Two reasons for the quantification of operational risk may be derived from the above explanation:

- To calculate the regulatory capital charge for operational risk and – in a second phase – to optimize the regulatory capital charge for operational risk.
- To manage the allocation of the bank owner's capital to achieve the optimal risk/reward combination.

Independent from the quantification method itself, the classification of risks needs to be exclusive. Otherwise the regulatory capital charge may be calculated twice; for example once for a credit risk and once for an operational risk. This situation should be avoided since it immediately affects the competitive position of the bank. The bank directly limits its commercial possibilities if it has to keep capital for risks it is not really exposed to.

The problem with the classification of risks is the scope of the observer. If the risk is observed based on its cause, the observer may classify the risk differently than an observer who looks to the effects of a risk. Many effects which occured in the last decade were financial losses in which derivative products were involved. If only the effect is observed, a classification as a market risk may be chosen. In most cases, however, the loss was caused by a human error or wrongly designed processes. If the cause of the loss is observed, the classification should be in the category of operational risk since the not-allowed positions could only exist due to a failing internal control system.

The same is true for the credit risk classification. If a customer is in default, it seems to be obvious that the resulting loss has been caused by a credit risk. It may be hard to say whether the loss really resulted from a credit risk rather than from an operational risk, and the following questions (not limited) may help in such an analysis:

- Have all procedures been adhered to during the approval of the credit?
- Was the credit analysis executed in compliance with all requirements and was all available data and information considered in the analysis process?
- Was the credit analysed in the predetermined cycle and did the credit committee approve these reviews on time?
- Did the bank adequately react to new information regarding the creditability of the customer?

If all these questions are answered positively the loss is assumed to be caused by credit risk. If failures in the internal control system are discovered based on these questions, which could have prevented the loss for the bank, the loss should be classified as caused by an operational risk.

These explanations make clear that a classification of losses based on the causes of risk is the only proper way to prevent double capital charges.

Another problem, which is still under discussion, is the complete coverage of operational risk for quantification purposes. Keck and Jovic (1999)[5] assume that operational risks can only be partly quantified, and they therefore propose to benchmark these operational risks against best practice according to the proposal of the Technical Committee of the International Organization of Securities. Dependent on the coverage of the benchmark, an 'add-on' should be calculated and added to the amount which results from the quantified operational risks. The operational risks meant are not explained by examples, but they are described as risks for which a loss potential cannot be derived and the probability cannot be calculated.

Quantification Methods Used

The quantification methods to achieve the capital allocation vary from simple methods which consider just one indicator, to sophisticated statistical

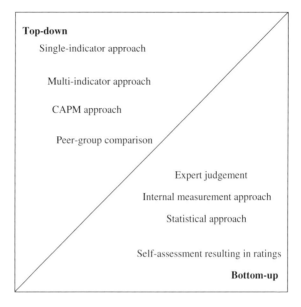

Figure 2.7　Top-down and bottom-up approaches

models. The methods can be classified as top-down or bottom-up approaches. In the case of a top-down approach, the capital charge is calculated on a group level and is then allocated to the business lines and products by using (simple) allocation keys. The bottom-up approach, however, analyses the operational risks on a single process level and then aggregates the risk numbers to a business line or a group level. The methods shown in Figure 2.7 will now be discussed.

Single-Indicator Approach

The single indicator approach is chosen as a start by the Basle Committee.[6] Just one indicator such as the total income of the bank, or the income volatility or total expenses is chosen and a predefined percentage of this variable is defined as the regulatory capital charge on a group level. The advantage of such a model is its simplicity. No complex calculations have to be made and data-collection processes almost diminish. Financial institutions with simple management information systems are also able to calculate their capital charge without any difficulties.

The Basle Committee[7] aligns the regulatory capital charge for operational risk to the approach of some banks. It was assumed by some banks that the regulatory capital charge for operational risk amounts to 20 per cent of current regulatory capital, and in its most recent document the Basle Committee did not want to change the regulatory capital charge for all risks on average. The possible positive effects of new calculation methods for credit risk are also absorbed for operational risk on the banking industry level. For individual banks, however, the regulatory capital charge may be lower or higher than under the old capital accord. The Basle Committee defined the following formula for the calculation of regulatory capital for operational risk (OR):

Regulatory capital charge OR $= \alpha \times$ gross income

The Basle Committee provisionally estimates the α-factor at 30 per cent. This percentage was to be set in after 2001.

But simplicity also has disadvantages. It is difficult to argue a causal relationship between the operational risks the bank is exposed to and the risk indicator chosen. Total expenses may relate to costs affected by staff and technology, and depreciation may represent the investments of the financial institution, but a causal relationship between the operational risk categories of people, systems and processes is hard to identify.

Financial institutions are also unable to differ between business lines. One business line can be properly organized and fully aware of the necessity of a control environment, whilst another business line may not be interested in these themes and is therefore poorly organized. Based on the single indicator approach, the financial institution's management is not able to remunerate the efforts of the business lines according to operational risk. The single indicator approach cannot be seen as an effective management tool for the management of the financial institution's scarcest resource: capital.

Multi-Indicator Approach (Standardized Approach)

The standardized approach is more focused on specific business lines in the financial institution; the approach acknowledges the different character of business within the bank. The regulator, however, still determines the regulatory capital charge.

In the consultative paper, the Basle Committee suggests mapping the financial institution's business to predetermined business lines. The indicators for operational risk per business line are predetermined as well. The business lines and indicators described in the Basle document[8] are shown in Table 2.1. These indicators are multiplied with a β-factor, which represents a rough estimate of the relationship between the industry's loss experience and the

Table 2.1   Business lines and indicators in the consultative document

Business units	Business lines	Indicator
Investment banking	Corporate finance	Gross income
	Trading and sales	Gross income[9]
Banking	Retail banking	Annual average assets
	Commercial banking	Annual average assets
	Payment and settlement	Annual settlement throughput
Others	Retail brokerage	Gross income
	Asset management	Total funds under management

Table 2.2   Relative weightings of the business lines

Business line	Range (%)
Corporate finance	8–12
Trading and sales	15–23
Retail banking	17–25
Commercial banking	13–20
Payment and settlement	12–18
Retail brokerage	6–9
Asset management	8–12
Total	80–120

broad financial indicator representing the bank's activity in a given business line, calibrated to a desired supervisory sound standard.

The relative weighting of each business line is described in ranges in the consultative document. The Basle Committee formulated the weightings in a range since it was not possible to analyse more exactly due to a lack of data. The relative weightings of the business lines proposed by the Basle Committee are shown in Table 2.2. The business lines 'insurance' and 'agency services' are not included in the proposal, although the final proposal is expected to include them.

The β-factor itself is calculated as follows:

$$\beta = \frac{[20\% \text{ current total MRC (\$)}] \times [\text{business line weighting (\%)}]}{\sum \text{ financial indicator for the business line from bank sample (\$)}}$$

where MRC = minimum capital charge.

The regulatory capital charge for a business line is calculated as follows:

Regulatory capital charge$_i = \beta_i \times$ indicator$_i$

The basic indicator approach can be used by all banks without any qualification. In the draft of the consultative paper of the European Commission, the basic indicator approach is not allowed as an alternative for internationally operating financial institutions. This is, however, not the case for the standardized approach. The following criteria are formulated by the Basle Committee:

- Effective management and control:

  - Independent risk control and audit function should exist.
  - Independent operational risk management and control process should exist.
  - Internal audit should regularly review the operational risk management process and measurement methodology.

- Measurement and validation:

  - Appropriate risk reporting systems to generate data used for the calculation of the capital charge.
  - Systematic tracking of relevant operational risk data by business line across the bank (loss data).
  - Development of specific documented criteria for mapping current business lines and activities to the standardized framework.

Although the standardized approach is an improvement in comparison to the basic indicator approach, it should be clear that the causal relationship between the operational risk in each business line and the regulatory capital charged for operational risk is still missing. The method can be executed without a sophisticated management information system, which could be a benefit for smaller banks as well.

The chosen indicators may even conflict with the performance management of the bank since the indicators chosen, such as gross income, should be maximized, although an increase of gross income would also lead to an increase of the regulatory capital charge. Moreover, a sound operational risk management, which may condense into a proper set of risk-mitigating measures, is not remunerated by this approach. Managers of business lines therefore do not have an incentive to implement proper control environments and a sound internal control and damage-control framework.

It is interesting to see the regulator requiring a tracking system for operational risk data by business line, although the losses caused by operational risk do not have a direct influence on the regulatory capital charge. It is fair to say that this data is crucial in the use of the internal measurement approach, and historical data for some (at this moment not exactly specified) years are required as a qualification for this approach.

A final point, which should be considered critically, is the need for a mapping to standard business lines. Although the reason for standard business lines may be found in avoiding a disturbance of current competitive relationships, the internal organization of financial institutions does not match to these standard business lines in most cases. This situation automatically reduces the value of this approach for internal management of the financial institution's capital.

CAPM Approach

The CAPM approach is based on the Capital Asset Pricing Model,[10] which is widely known in the finance industry. This model describes a relationship between the risk and return in an efficient market. The focus of this book is the operational risk of a financial institution, and in this view only β[11] is interesting. The financial institution is seen as a portfolio; it is assumed that a single stockholder would possess all stocks of the company. In this case the stockholder would run the full business risk of the company, and β_{asset} then reflects the whole hypothetical portfolio. The $\beta_{portfolio}$ is the weighted average of the debt and the equity betas:

$$\beta_{asset} = \beta_{portfolio} = \left\{ \beta_{dept} \times \frac{dept}{dept + equity} \right\} + \left\{ \beta_{equity} \times \frac{equity}{debt + equity} \right\}$$

A firm's asset β reflects its business risk. The difference between the firm's equity β and asset β reflects its financial risk, since more debt implies more financial risk. Operational risk could be reflected by the asset β.

This method of quantifying operational risk is not widely adopted in the banking industry, although the first experiences were made in the early development stages by Chase Manhattan Bank. The following problems may be the cause of the lack of recognition by supervisors and financial institutions:

• The value of the method for internal measurement of operational risk is quite low, since a decomposition of the calculated operational risk to business lines and processes is hardly possible.

- The business risk represented by β_{asset} is not comparable to the operational risk of a financial institution. Operational risk should be seen as a subset of the business risk.

Peer-Group Comparison

Peer-group comparison is based on benchmarking among various financial institutions considering public information such as balance sheet totals, gross income, gross result and transaction volumes. It is clear that the transformation of these parameters to a risk-exposure amount is still more an art rather than based on verifiable procedures. This method is quite close to the single-indicator approach and therefore contains the same weaknesses. The difference is mainly in the relativity of the approach, since the information of the various financial institutions is seen in relationship to each other.

Expert Judgement

The basis for an expert judgement is a scenario analysis; experts estimate the expected risk amounts and the probabilities of occurrence. Expert judgement is seen as a good alternative if data collection is not easy or the data available are insufficient for an adequate statistical analysis. The latter may be true for some corporate finance activities, since the financial institution closes a relatively small number of merger & acquisition transactions. If these transactions are analysed, the result may be that no loss is found, but the operational risk which is inherent to this transaction type should not be estimated as zero. It would be quite helpful if experts would estimate the operational risk involved based on a well-defined scenario and their special knowledge. They will be able to identify 'near-accidents' and risks which are not directly clear for an external observer.

The scenarios, however, should be defined very carefully. They should be clear; all experts should use the same product definitions, the same procedures and the scenario as such should not be differently interpretable due to its wording. Quality checks on the scenarios themselves should not be omitted. It would be advisable to use the same criteria for an expert judgement round as in the scientific approach to laboratory empirical research. Experts other than the experts who will be involved in the final judgement should execute the pilot of the scenarios.

Even if the experts are confronted with well-prepared scenarios, they may judge the risk exposure and the probabilities of occurrence differently. Experts are still influenced by their reference framework, which consists of knowledge and – more importantly – experiences. Experiences are often accompanied by emotions, which may bias the judgement of the expert. It depends on the method used whether these biases can be identified. Sometimes expert judgements are organized as round-table discussions; a professional moderation of these discussions could help to identify biases, if any. If the expert judgements are delivered only in written form, the scenarios should be specially designed to be able to identify any influences of biases.

It should be noted that the form of the expert judgement may influence the results. The 'round-table' format can result in an 'on average' judgement, since people have a natural attitude to look for consent. In the case of risk exposure this approach can be particularly dangerous. Some experts may see higher exposures, but they are probably not able to defend their judgement rationally. A worse case would be where political correctness forces certain experts to judge the risk exposure more favourably than a good reflection of reality would allow. The participants should therefore be carefully chosen.

In large financial institutions scenarios may be made anonymous and judged by experts who are not directly involved in the described scenario. As soon as experts recognize that they are involved in the scenario, they may judge subjectively in order to mitigate consequences (the final consequence could be a higher capital allocation!). It should also be ensured that each expert judgement is included in the analysis before the experts take note of each other's judgements. The bandwidth of the judgements should also be made transparent in the analysis. A second round should verify the results of the first round, since risk exposure should not be based on average judgements, but on well-accepted maximum scenarios.

Contrary to the other methods, the calculation of the risk exposure is a little bit easier since the parameters are directly inquired into.

Internal Measurement Approach

The Basle Committee suggests the internal measurement approach as a more advanced method to calculate the regulatory capital charge. The supervisor still defines the calculation method, whereas the internal loss data of the financial institutions are considered. As described for the standardized approach, the financial institution's activities are mapped to standard business lines defined by the supervisor. In the consultative paper the Basle Committee[12] suggested the loss types shown in Table 2.3.

It should be noted that the risk types are effect-driven. If a financial institution is only mapping its losses to these risk types some interesting

Table 2.3   Risk types according to the Basle Committee

Risk type	Contents
Write-downs	Theft, fraud, unauthorized activity, market and credit losses arising as a result of operational events
Loss of recourse	Payments or disbursements made to incorrect parties and not recovered
Restitution	Payments to clients of principal and/or interest by way of restitution, or the cost of any form of compensation paid to clients
Legal liability	Judgements, settlements and other legal costs
Regulatory and compliance	Fines, or other direct costs of any penalties, such as licence revocations
Loss of or damage to assets	Direct reduction in value of physical assets, including certificates, due to some kind of accident (e.g. neglect, accident, fire, earthquake)

information is lost. The cause of the risk in particular should be investigated, since improvement of the risk profile of the financial institution is only possible if this cause can be stopped. If the risk may only be mitigated by insurance, the insurers could have an interest in the risk profile of the financial institution in order to offer a better-fitting coverage and premium than they could have offered without this knowledge.

The supervisor[13] specifies an exposure indicator (EI) per business line/risk-type combination. This exposure indicator is a proxy for the size or amount of risk of each business line's operational risk exposure. The internal loss data of the financial institution, the probability of a loss event (PE), should be derived as well as the parameter 'loss given that event' (LGE). The expected loss of each business line/risk-type combination is calculated as:

$$EL = EI \times PE \times LGE$$

The supervisor defines the γ-factor for each business line/risk-type combination, which translates the expected loss into a capital charge. The γ-factor will be determined based on an industry-wide loss distribution. The overall regulatory capital charge for a financial institution is calculated as:

$$\text{regulatory capital charge} = \sum_{i} \sum_{j} \left[\gamma(i, j) \times EI\,(i, j) \times PE(i, j) \times LGE(i, j) \right]$$

where i is the business line and j is the risk type.

All parameters have to be disclosed to the supervisor in order to ensure a standard calculation of regulatory capital charges throughout the banking industry. The business lines used for the internal measurement approach are the same as those used for the standardized approach (see Table 2.2).

The Basle Committee formulated the following qualifying criteria for the use of the internal measurement approach:

- Effective risk and management control:

    o Accuracy of loss data and confidence in the results of calculations have to be established through 'use tests'.

- Measurement and validation:

    o Sound internal loss reporting practices consistent with the scope of operational losses as defined by supervisors.
    o Operational risk-management methodology, knowledgeable staff and appropriate systems for loss-data collection and the calculation of PE and LGE should be available.
    o Loss data should be available over a number of years (not exactly defined), and criteria for assigning losses to business lines and risk types should be formulated.
    o A sound process to identify the events used to construct a database and identify which historical loss experiences are appropriate for the institution.
    o Rigorous conditions for supplementing external loss data to internal data sources of external data need to be reviewed regularly.
    o Banks must regularly validate their loss rates, risk indicators and size estimations.
    o Scenario analysis and stress testing is seen as helpful to check if the operational environment is adequately reflected.
    o The bank's management should incorporate experience and judgement into an analysis of the loss data and the resulting PEs and LGEs.

It should be noted that the qualifying requirements are additional to the requirements for the standardized approach.

The internal measurement approach has some significant advantages in comparison to the standardized approach. First of all the bank's own historical loss data are considered and therefore the bank will be able to use its competitive benefits. If the bank's investments in sound processes are reflected in lower historical losses, the bank is able to use a greater part of its capital base for commercial activities than could a financial institution whose first priority was other themes rather than sound processes. The financial institution's regulatory capital charge is based on a causal relationship with the losses which have occurred.

Although the internal measurement approach shows advantages, it has some disadvantages as well:

- The standardized business lines as set by the supervisor may not match the internal business lines in the organization. As seen by the standardized approach, reconciliation of the management accounts with the financial accounts may therefore be more difficult.
- The loss types as presented in Table 2.3 may not match the internally-defined loss types. The granularity of the set loss types by the Basle Committee may not be sufficient for internal management purposes. A mapping process seems to be unavoidable here as well.
- The approach is bottom-up and therefore labour-intensive. The collection of the loss data per risk type may be especially difficult. Losses are sometimes not booked in special error accounts and it may be hard to discover the cause of the loss. The requirements of a loss database will be discussed in a separate section.

The Basle Committee expects that financial institutions will move along the approaches over time, and it is expected that these approaches will result in a lower regulatory capital charge for the financial institutions. In its Consultative Document the Basle Committee considers a 'floor' below which the regulatory capital charge should not fall. Two approaches are presented:

- A fixed percentage for the regulatory capital charge as calculated under the standardized approach.
- Minimum levels for elements of the expected loss (EL) calculation based on the industry-wide loss data and distributions.

The Basle Committee acknowledges that both methods are crude. The first method may suggest that the standardized approach is a more reliable measure of operational risk than the internal measurement approach. The second method relies on a broad supervisory judgement.

Statistical Approaches

Analogous to quantification methods for market risk and, more recently, also credit risk, statistical methods for operational risk were researched.

Contrary to market risk, it is difficult to reach a representative statistical model. Before the statistical methods are discussed, the problems regarding the quality and availability of data will be considered.

Loss data issues Regarding loss data the following issues can be formulated:

- The loss cases are not independent of each other.
- The losses are sometimes not properly recorded, for example failing data.
- The number of loss cases is too small to conduct a classical statistical analysis.
- Especially losses in the category 'high impact, low frequency' are internally not available.

Loss cases are not independent of each other since one loss case may cause the next. For example, a system error may cause many corrective actions which have to be performed by employees under high time pressure. The resulting stress may be the cause of additional errors. If the system error had been avoided, all false corrective actions would not have occurred. This issue should be considered in the case of quantification and statistical analysis.

Losses are sometimes not properly recorded. First of all staff are not eager to explain to superiors that they have made a loss, and therefore they might try to hide the loss by booking it in profit and loss accounts with many movements. Particularly in the case of penalty interest may staff find an easy way to book the loss in the main interest accounts. Even if the losses are properly booked in separate error accounts, the information available in accounting entries may be insufficient. The booking date is, for example, not of interest, but the date on which the loss was caused is. The cause of the loss, the steps taken afterwards, and many other interesting details will not be available in the accounting entries.

In order to obtain proper loss data collection, at least the following properties of a loss case should be recorded:

- The loss amount.
- The product involved.
- The occurrence date.
- The cause of the loss.
- A description of the loss.
- The process step in which the loss occurred.

- The loss category.
- Cascade effects if any.

It is clear that the proposed list is a bare minimum. These data may be enriched with a workflow in order to document the loss sign-off process more effectively. If the accounting entry on the error accounts is generated by the loss recording system, a matching between the loss database and the general ledger is guaranteed.

It has still not been clarified which losses have to be recorded, and the following questions need to be answered:

- Should only financial losses with a direct negative impact to the profit and loss account be recorded?
- Should 'near-accidents' be recorded as well, and if so which loss amount should be included?
- Which loss amount should be recorded in the case of indirect losses and reputation losses (as far as the financial institution is able to recognize)? Should it be the opportunity loss?

These questions are not resolved at this moment, and are also not finally addressed in the consultative paper of the Basle Committee.

The last issue to be addressed is the lack of data in internal loss cases in the category 'high impact, low frequency'. The loss cases can be plotted as shown in Figure 2.8.

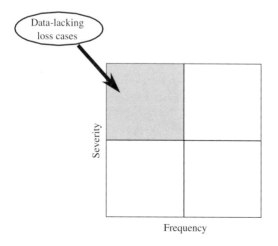

Figure 2.8   Data-lacking loss cases

Data-lacking losses may be included by using external data, and Robert Ceske[14] *et al.* (2000) have explained the use of external data. External data cannot be easily used, however, since they have to be shaped to the size of the organization. The causes also need to be analysed, since the financial institution considered should only take those loss data into account which apply to the institution's business. For that reason, the Basle Committee[15] also requires a sound procedure for the inclusion of external losses if the financial institution likes to include external data in its statistical approach (which is already the case in the internal measurement approach).

A statistical approach   After completing the most important step in the quantitative analysis – the data-collection part – a statistical analysis can be conducted. Ceske *et al.* (2000) perform the following steps in their statistical approach:

• The loss data is plotted in a frequency–severity graph (see Figure 2.9).
• Based on the graph the use of a distribution is decided; it is possible to choose different distributions for the various parts of the graph.
• For the 'tail' of the graph the use of the extreme value theory is suggested.

The tail of the graph represents high losses with a low frequency, which could be fitted using the extreme value theory. Even if all losses of the banking industry could be collected, the number of extreme cases may still

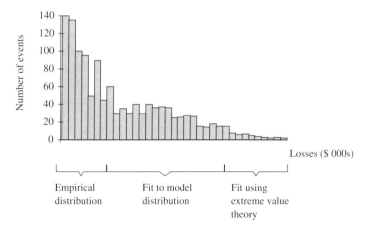

Figure 2.9 Severity of loss events on a logarithmic scale

$$G_{\xi,\mu,\beta}(x) = \begin{cases} 1 - \left(1 + \xi\,\dfrac{x-\mu}{\beta}\right)^{-1/\xi} & for\ \xi \neq 0 \\[2ex] 1 - \exp\left(-\dfrac{x-\mu}{\beta}\right) & for\ \xi = 0 \end{cases}$$

Loss ← ┐
Shape- ← ┘
factor

Figure 2.10   Extreme value theory calculations

be too small for a classic statistical analysis. The shaping of the graph is executed using the equations shown in Figure 2.10. The approach as such is based on statistical science. However, it should be considered that some steps with a rather artificial flavour have been taken in order to reach a statistical distribution. The practical value of this model should be proven by back-testing. As long as most loss databases do not contain enough historical data, it is too early to evaluate the model for practical usage.

Value at risk for operational risks   Reinhard Buhr (2000)[16] describes an approach for the calculation of a value at risk for operational risk. The positive effect of the approach is the possibility of adding the value-at-risk numbers for credit risk, market risk and operational risk to achieve a risk value for a certain business line of a financial institution. Buhr defines value at risk as: *the assumed largest negative value change of a portfolio in a certain time frame, which is needed to close or sell the considered risk position under a given confidence level.*

The method is a real bottom-up approach, since it analyses all relevant processes in detail. The internal control measures are identified as control points. For each control point the maximal damage is estimated in the case of a failing control; the probability of a failing control is also estimated. Both parameters will be the basis for a value-at-risk calculation; the multiplication of the two parameters results in a value-at-risk number for the specific control point.

If the value at risk for operational risk is to be aggregated at a bank level, it should be considered that a loss may be caused by more than simply one failing internal control point. The following scenarios could be possible:

• The losses are independent of each other.
• The specific loss is a subset of other losses.
• The specific loss may be dependent on other losses.

The dependencies of losses are expressed in a correlation matrix; losses which are a subset of other losses are summarized in a cluster.

Control point C208 FX-trading	Max. rating MRi	Actual rating ARi	Actual weighting AWi	Max. Score MSi	Actual Score ASi	Scale % S%I
1	4	1	1	16	4	25%
2	4	3	3	12	9	75%
3	4	2	2	8	2	50%
4	4	1	2	8	4	25%
Aggregated	MRxAW=MS				43%	43%
5	4	4	4	16	16	100%
6	4	1	1	4	1	25%
7	4	4	1	4	4	100%
8	4	2	2	8	4	50%
9	4	3	2	8	6	75%
10	4	2	2	8	4	50%
11	4	4	2	8	8	100%
Aggregated					71%	76%
Total	ARxAW=AS				61%	62%

Callouts: S% =AR/MR · Weighted Average 5% · Average 5%

Figure 2.11   Internal control cluster matrix

The value-at-risk (*VaR*) number at the cluster level is calculated as follows:

$$VaR \text{ cluster} = \sqrt{(X, YX)}$$

VaR (single control point) correlationmatrix (containing all control points)

The calculation of the aggregated value at risk is conducted using the same formula, using the correlations of all single losses. Buhr pointed out that just an addition of the value-at-risk amount for the single control points is acceptable as a starting point in order to reach a number at the bank level. Further developments of this method are expected in the future.

This method closely focuses on processes; the human, system and external risks are not really considered in this method. It may be possible to enrich the described method with both risk types in order to reach a complete coverage of operational risk. The consideration of dependencies is seen a positive step, since especially in the case of operational risk a specific error may cause the next one.

Quantification of people risk   Deloitte & Touche (1999)[17] developed a method to quantify people risk, the categories of which are shown in Figure 2.12. The method proposed uses various statistical approaches which are conducted dependently to the risk type. The risk of theft and fraud has a different form than the risk of insufficient qualifications of staff, for example. A practical approach has been chosen to solve this issue. The fraud risk has been displayed by using fuzzy logic techniques, since this risk has no statistical behaviour. The insufficient qualification of

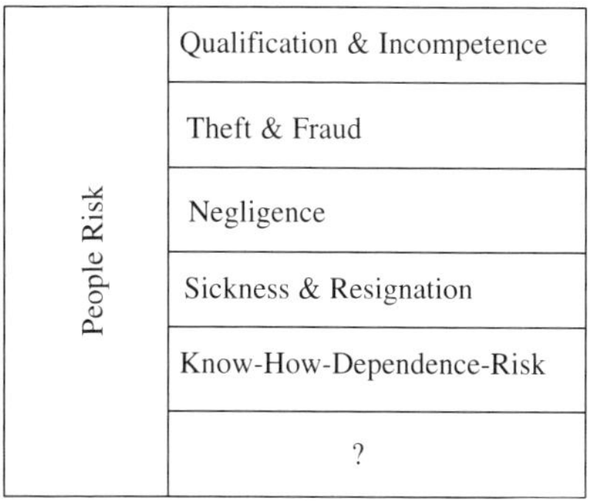

People Risk	Qualification & Incompetence
	Theft & Fraud
	Negligence
	Sickness & Resignation
	Know-How-Dependence-Risk
	?

Figure 2.12   People risk

Source: Deloitte & Touche (1999).

staff has been modelled by a β-distribution from a Monte Carlo simulation using a confidence level of 97.5 per cent. The holding period for this simulation was set as one year. The holding period is an issue: in the case of market risks the holding period is seen as the time necessary to close an open position. For operational risk, however, the time horizon is not so interesting. The relatively long period has probably been chosen to avoid a small number of loss cases regarding the mentioned risk.

For each risk category so called 'risk numbers' are calculated which are added to obtain a risk number on the people's risk level. A critical issue in this situation is also the correlation of the single risks. This correlation effect can only be recognized in this method by direct entry of an estimate of the correlation value.

Event tree   The quantification of operational risk can be conducted using the various methods discussed. In order to construct a model that fits operational risk quantification the loss-causing events have to be researched. In Chapter 1 the risks have been described. The next step could be research into the possible combinations of events. Such combinations of events can be represented diagrammatically as 'trees', each tree linking various events by its branches.

As soon as event trees have been designed, the probability of each combination of events should be estimated. A possible question could be: 'What is the probability that a human error is followed by a system error?' This type of question can be asked for each combination. It should still be noticed that the availability of data limits the use of statistical methods. It should therefore be considered whether data originating from equivalent events can be used in the analysis. If direct data collection is not possible, it may be reasonable for data from equivalent events to be used.

As soon as the event structure has been defined, the statistical analysis should follow as the next step, the method chosen being dependent on the availability of data. If there are enough cases, classical statistical analysis can be conducted, but in most cases a Bayesian approach may be more reasonable. The last step is the calculation of the expected loss resulting from operational risk and exposure, which should be based on a value-at-risk concept. The events which may cause a loss should be defined, and in this section the possible relationships between the events are also described. The events are generically described; it should be further researched whether a generic description fits or whether specific events have to be defined for each business line. The formulated relationships should be seen as assisting in the design of an own model.

The loss-causing events can be generically defined as in Table 2.4. All events which are described are internal events. The external influences which cause an operational risk are excluded in this phase, since it is not clear how these issues are covered in the model.

One error may cause another error. For example a human processing error may cause a disruption of the end-of-day process, so that some reports may be based on incomplete data and may cause decision errors. In real life, for example, a call money contract may be wrongly entered in the processing system and therefore the interest-calculation module is not able to calculate the interest amounts of all contracts. Non-calculated values cannot be included in reports and the user of reports may draw false conclusions, which can result in losses.

Table 2.4   Loss-causing events

Human processing error	An unconscious human error which can result in a direct loss, a system error or a decision error
Human decision error	A human decision error which is caused by incomplete, wrong or unavailable information
System error	An unexpected event which results in a disruption of system processes or in an incomplete or incorrect execution of system processes. The events can occur autonomously or can be caused by human imperfection
Process design error	An inadequate design of a process may result in human processing errors, system errors and they may also lead to fraud
Fraud	A conscious human error which is actively performed to damage the financial institution

A distinction between errors and fraud should be made since the probability of a financial loss is larger in fraud than in the case of an error. An overview of possible relationships between errors is included in Appendix 2; for some of these relationships examples are presented below:

- *Human processing error →financial/reputation loss*

  o A payment order has been charged to the wrong account; the balance on this account is not sufficient for a correction.
  o A securities order has been processed too late and the bank is confronted with an interest claim.

- *Human processing error →human decision error →financial/ reputation loss*

  o A false assignment of a transaction to the customer's limit causes an unnecessary rejection of a profitable transaction by the risk manager.

- *Human processing error →system error →financial/reputation loss*

  o Wrongly entered transactions in the processing system cause disruption of batch-processes and therefore the accounting entries are not executed. Clients dispose incorrectly and confront the bank with an interest claim.
  o Files are not labelled as 'processed' due to a human error and therefore double processing is executed. Even if a correction is performed on time, the error and the correction are printed in the account statements.

- *Human processing error →system error →human decision error → financial/reputation loss*

  o Reports include incomplete information, since incomplete data entry disrupts a certain process in the end-of-day batch. Based on this report the money-market trader funds a too small amount, which causes problems in the clearing system.

- *System error →financial/reputation loss*

  o Due to a system error the account statements are not available.
  o The standing orders are not executed due to a system error. Clients confront the bank with an interest claim for late payments.

- *System error → human processing error→ financial/reputation loss*

  ○ A system error causes many manual corrections. Since these corrections are performed under high time pressure, new errors exist, which cause financial damage.

- *System error → human processing error → human decision error → financial/reputation loss*

  ○ A system error causes many manual corrections. Since these corrections are performed under high time pressure, new errors occur which cause an inadequate liquidity report. The money-market trader funds a wrong amount and the bank has to use its credit line with the central bank in order to perform in the clearing process. An interest loss is caused since the interest charge of the central bank is higher than the normal interest charges for money-market transactions.

- *System error → human decision error → financial/reputation loss*

  ○ A disruption of the front-office system causes a delay in the information supply to the trader. The market is quite volatile in that moment, and the trader is unable to rephrase his strategy since he does not know his current position and the bank will therefore be confronted with unnecessary losses.

- *Process design error → financial/reputation loss*

  ○ An ill-designed process causes errors which cause losses to the bank. All accounting entries are performed one day earlier than necessary and therefore cause an interest loss.

- *Process design error → human processing error → financial/reputation loss*

  ○ The process is not clearly designed and therefore staff interpret the process step wrongly. The wrong interpretation causes damage.

- *Process design error → human processing error → human decision error → financial/reputation loss*

  ○ The process is not clearly designed and therefore staff interpret the process step wrongly. The wrong interpretation causes inaccurate data entries, and some reports are therefore incomplete. The decisions based on these reports cause losses.

The other relationships may be analysed analogously. If an analysis is performed the fit of the relationships to the processes in the organization should be investigated.

A model for a process with many transactions   The model to be presented could be a starting point for the measurement of operational risk in a high transactional volume area of a financial institution. This model is still in its pilot phase. The first proof of concept was performed for payment processes, and therefore some features of the model are characteristic of payment services. The model has the following properties:

- Risk indicators are defined for each process step.
- For each risk indicator probabilities are defined. The probabilities are preferably based on empirical data, or expert opinions are used to estimate probabilities. Since the processing of payment orders needs to be completed before a so-called cut-off time, it is supposed that the error rates increase as soon as the transaction volume increases.
- The loss scenario is defined as follows:

  o   The error is not discovered.
  o   The error is not correctly adjusted.

- The probability that an error is not discovered increases if the transaction volume increases.
- The probability that a discovered error cannot be adjusted on time increases if the remaining time before the cut-off time decreases.
- Each loss scenario receives a mean severity of consequence, which is the average financial loss which is to be expected per loss scenario.

The result of the model in a graph which indicates the probability of higher loss than the risk exposure caused by operational risk. The displayed graph is a result of the analysis of the process 'outgoing mass payments' (Figure 2.13). All process steps are analysed and the risks are defined per category. The loss amounts are randomly chosen, to avoid any recognition of the financial institution which delivered the process.

The day has been cut into five periods since the transactions have to be final before certain cut-off times. Based on these periods the transaction volume is also divided. The probability of the detection and recovery of errors is dependent on the transaction volumes per period. The graph should be read as follows: the probability that a daily loss is higher than DM 10 000 (1.00E+04) is about 10% (1.00E−01).

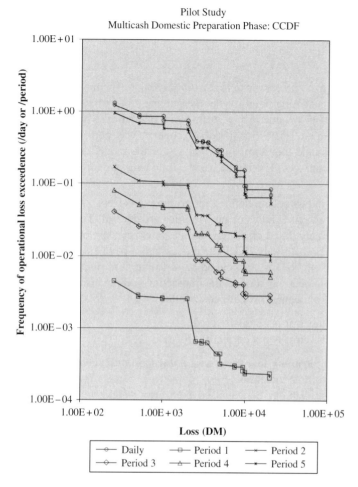

Figure 2.13   The results of an operational risk model

The method is quite close to the value-at-risk concept, which is used for the valuation of market risk. The only difference is that a confidence level is not included in this approach. As soon as the pilot phase is concluded, a confidence level will also be included in this model. The model can be easily adapted to transaction banking practice; however, operational risk exists not only in the back office of a financial institution, but in all areas where people, systems and processes play a role.

Self-Assessment Resulting in Ratings

A self-assessment is one of the bottom-up approaches which can also be used for the quantification of operational risk. Although the approach is qualitative, a quantification is possible as long as experts give an overview of the risk exposure and the probability of the risk. Since each risk is not equally important, the self-assessor is asked to weight the answers (relevance). If all inquiries are analysed the result will be a risk amount regarding operational risk.

The inquiries are close to the self-diagnosis process described earlier. It is a complex balancing act to cover all operational risks on the one hand, and to keep a practical approach on the other. The number of questions cannot be unlimited, since too many questions could affect the acceptance of the process by the self-assessors. This method seems not to be sophisticated, but it should be considered that it delivers a scope to the operational risk problem which allows management to plan corrective actions. The relationship between the loss and the risk is clearer than in some statistical approaches. It should not be forgotten that the loss distribution as shown before, does not allow a trace back to the cause of the loss. The input of external data complicates this tracing even more. Operational risk management is not only a capital allocation issue: the mitigation of operational risk should be the main focus of all analysis.

Concluding Remark

The overview of the quantification methods used for operational risk shows a huge effort has been made by scientists and practitioners to make progress, which should result in a financial institution-wide approach. Based on the research performed, however, it is fair to say there is still a long way to go before that target is reached.

Discussion about the value of a statistical approach has still not been concluded. Some experts doubt its value for the management of operational risk since tracking back from the loss to the loss-causing risk is in some cases not valid. In our view the mono-approach should not be taken, since too much information would not be made transparent if only a statistical approach were chosen. For capital allocation purposes, however, some quantification method needs to be used.

An Intermezzo: The Adviser's Risk

In Germany, relationship managers are required by law to clarify the risks of financial products to their customers. The risks need to be clarified in

such a way that the customer is himself able to oversee the risks involved
in the financial products.

Clients are classified according to their knowledge and experience, and
the classifications are related to product categories which may be traded if
the customer proves his knowledge and experience. An important difference among the various classes is the allowance to trade forward products.
Many banks use the classes shown in Table 2.5.

A distinction should be made between advisory portfolio management
and discretionary portfolio management in the case of private banking. If
the bank performs advisory portfolio management, the relationship manager advises the customer, but the customer decides himself whether to
invest accordingly or not. If the customer gives a discretionary portfolio
management order, the customer sets the conditions in which the adviser is
allowed to invest the money. The customer may, for example, determine
that investment should only be in western European currencies. However,
the client is not requested to authorize every single transaction.

The various financial instruments also need to be classified to be able to
quantify the adviser's risk. A government bond has quite a lower risk profile
than a warrant on an Adidas share. This classification cannot easily be
performed for structured products. In Germany the so called 'Aktienanleihe'

Table 2.5   Knowledge classification

Knowledge class	Products
A	For example deposits, government debt, money-market funds. Investment strategy: defensive
B	A and e.g. bank bonds, real-estate funds. Investment strategy: conservative
C	B and e.g. other local currency bonds, interest-oriented investment funds. Investment strategy: moderate conservative
D	C and e.g. mixed funds, convertibles and foreign-exchange and option-related bonds. Investment strategy: growth-oriented
E	D and e.g. stock, stock funds. Investment strategy: managed risk
F	E and e.g. warrants, other forward trades. Investment strategy: speculative

Note: For class F the client is also requested to indicate his experience with investments
in securities.

Source: Comdirect bank AG.

(a bond combined with an option on shares) was quite popular; the bond was repaid in cash or, if the option had been exercised, by shares. The interest on the bond was very high, containing the option premium. At the introduction of the product it was classified as a bond. As soon as the first products needed to be repaid, investors were embarrassed since they became shares with a market value lower than the nominal value of the bond. Investors started to file, saying that the relationship managers had not informed them about the risks involved. The description 'bond' was misleading according to the investors. Although the cases looked promising, it was decided in court that customers did not need to be classified in class F to be allowed to trade the structured product.

Another prerequisite for the quantification of the adviser's risk is the identification of risks. The following risks may occur:

- The relationship manager does not exactly explain the inherent risks of the investment to the customer.
- The relationship manager does not request a written declaration of the customer's knowledge and experience.
- The relationship manager executes a security order which does not fit the customer's knowledge and experience profile.
- The customer executes a security order via online banking which does not match to his knowledge and experience.
- The relationship manager executes a security order under a discretionary portfolio management order which does not comply with the principles of this order.
- The customer-support department enters the customer in an incorrect knowledge and experience class; the customer is therefore authorized to trade products with a higher risk profile than allowed.
- The bank's system does not check before the security order is executed whether the customer is allowed to trade the security according to his knowledge and experience class.

It is clear that a financial institution likes to avoid or minimize the mentioned risks and it may have implemented adequate internal controls. Examples of internal controls are:

- The custody account is blocked until the customer signs off a declaration of his knowledge and experience.
- The advice to the customer is supported with documents which additionally make clear the inherent risk profile of the various products.
- The knowledge and experience class of the customer is entered in a supporting system. For the execution of each security order the system

checks whether the customer is allowed to. The data entry of the class is verified by a second staff member.

- The bank will promote additional training to support the relationship manager with knowledge of new products and their features. Training may avoid a situation where the relationship manager advises the client inappropriately without perceiving the sub-optimal quality of his advice.

If the customer's knowledge and experience is properly recorded in the system and the financial instruments are classified, an analysis of the custody accounts of all customers would discover unmatched positions, if any. Customers who have traded a financial instrument which does not match their classification represent a potential adviser's risk of the bank. These accounts should be further investigated. A detailed investigation should detect the following:

- In which cases and under which circumstances was the financial institution confronted with a claim regarding the adviser's risk? To what amount did the bank suffer a loss? Not only filed cases are interesting for this analysis, cases which were settled between the customer and the financial institution should also be included.
- The volatility of the financial instruments should also be included in the analysis.

The expected loss per customer is dependent on:

- the probability that the investment is loss-making for the customer (the higher the volatility, the higher the probability of a loss);
- the probability that the customer will make the financial institution liable for the loss;
- the probability that key controls will fail in a critical moment; and
- the maximal damage amount.

The expected loss for the financial institution is equal to the sum of all expected losses per customer. No covariance effects exist within one custody account since the customer may sue the financial institution for each single financial instrument in his custody account. Equally, no covariance effects exist if the risk on the financial institution's level is calculated, since each customer decides singularly whether he makes the financial institution liable for the loss-making investment.

The probability that the customer files his case depends especially on the chance of a positive judgement in court and the personal situation of the customer. In some cases, case law already exists, which may stimulate customers to file their cases. However, if a customer wishes to avoid certain investments becoming known, he may decide not to file his case. Moreover, the loss amount itself may influence the probability of whether a case will be filed or not. If the loss amount is relatively small, the customer is probably willing not to file. In the case of a high loss with a substantial impact on the customer's wealth, the customer needs to file a case. It is hard for a financial institution to model the described decision-making on the customer's side, since the bank does not always oversee the complete financial situation of the customer. For practical reasons, the probability of a filed case by the customer should only be based on the volatility of the financial instruments included in his custody account.

The managing board of a private bank may primarily be interested in an analysis of the existing situation. First of all the threatening losses and the resulting filed cases in the existing assets under management should be detected. In this case the probability of failing internal controls are not interesting, since in the case of a mismatch between the customer's investments and his classification, the internal controls actually did fail.

The expected loss amount can be calculated as follows:

Expected loss = probability of a filed case × probability VaR × value-at-risk financial investment

If the expected losses for all custody accounts are added, the result is the expected loss for the financial institution. Summarizing, the process may be represented as in Figure 2.14.

As a second step a model can be designed for the adviser's risk of the financial institution. The probability of failing internal controls should also be taken into account. If the incidents or at least the losses are properly recorded by the financial institution, this could be a basis for the estimation of the probability of failing internal controls. If such a registration fails, it should be replaced by an expert's judgement.

CAPITAL ALLOCATION

The quantification of operational risk is a prerequisite for capital allocation on the various business lines. This prerequisite is a logical consequence of the performance measurement of products and services offered by financial institutions. The performance indicator 'return on solvency' (ROS) was firstly implemented in the USA as capital in financial institutions became

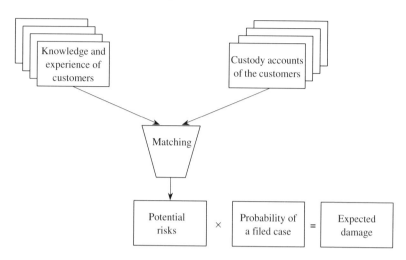

Figure 2.14   Analysis of the adviser's risk

scarce. The process of choosing alternatives became important since banks needed to optimize their capital allocation to maximize the return per risk capital unit. Not only single transactions are objects of the optimization process, but also the contribution of complete business lines to the financial institution's financial result. The contributions of each business unit should be made comparable.

The regulatory capital allocation is quite different per business line. In the business line 'private banking', ROS numbers of more than 60 per cent are quite common since private banking business does not involve much regulatory capital. Corporate banking business, however, should be considered differently, since much regulatory capital is required for the classical lending business.

The payment service examples are very interesting from an operational risk point of view. Payment services do not require much regulatory capital under the current regulatory capital requirements; if cash flows are perfectly managed, such capital is not needed for the debit balances on nostro accounts. In other words, payment services do not expose the bank to credit and market risk and therefore a regulatory capital charge is currently not required for payment services. If the scope is enlarged to operational risk as well, a regulatory capital for payment services is required. Operational risk plays an important role in the payment services department. It should be noticed that the basic indicator approach as proposed by the Basle Committee does not cover payment services completely, since it is quite hard to determine the gross income resulting from payment transactions. In some banks, the payment transactions as such are free as long as they are offered through on-line banking to the financial institution. The basic indicator 'gross income' is therefore not adequate for the representation of operational risk within the payment services department.

Before the Basle Committee fixed the regulatory capital charge as 20 per cent of the minimum required capital, some operational risk experts published estimates of the operational risk regulatory capital charge. Michel Crouhy (1998)[18] estimates the portion of capital charge for operational risk at 20 per cent with a tendency to 30 per cent. For market risk the capital charge is estimated in a bandwith between 10 per cent and 30 per cent. The increase is expected to be compensated by a decrease in the capital portion for credit risk. It is expected that operational risk will increase in the future and therefore an upwards tendency is estimated. The authors expect an increased staff fluctuation in financial institutions, an increasing product complexity, increasing transaction volumes, a quick introduction of new technologies and more mergers between, or acquisitions of, financial institutions. Hugo Everts (1999)[19] expects the economic capital for operational risk in the range 10–25 per cent. Economic capital is based on an internal analysis of the capital needed for each business line, and is therefore not equal to regulatory capital. The percentages, however, clearly show that operational risk is at least equally weighted to market risk. The basis for these estimations is not described in the mentioned literature, but based on the research of the Basle Committee it is accepted in the banking industry. As soon as a better quantification method has been introduced, it is expected that the basis may be reviewed as well.

The portion of regulatory capital for operational risk should be allocated to the various business lines. The allocation key should be objective and may be determined based on the following questions:

- To which inherent risk is the business line exposed?
- Are adequate internal control measures implemented to mitigate operational risk?
- What is the development of the operational risk indicators (such as staff turnover)?
- What track record of loss is available for the business line?

These questions already show that an objective allocation method for regulatory capital may not easily be found.

Most capital allocation methods are based on the economic capital concept. Jovic (1999)[20] defines economic capital as equity capital which must be held to support that particular level of risky business activity. Economic capital therefore includes all relevant risks to which the financial institution is exposed. Economic capital is based on a value-at-risk concept acording to Jovic. Based on the graph shown in Figure 2.15, it can be concluded that the economic capital portion covers the unexpected loss (under a given confidence level and holding period).

The amount of economic capital needed depends on the risk appetite of the financial institution's management. The management may decide to set the amount equal to the value-at-risk amount, which is statistically correct. But, as mentioned, the confidence level already indicates that a loss can on occasion be higher than the value-at-risk value. Prudent management may then decide to set the economic capital amount higher than just the value-at-risk amount. The default rate can also be the basis for the expansion of the level of economic capital. The default rate, which expresses the risk appetite of the financial institution, is the basis for the determination of the corresponding quantile α_d. The following formula can be used to calculate the economic capital:

$$\text{economic capital} = \frac{\alpha_d \times VaR}{\alpha_{VaR}}$$

where α_d = quantile based on the chosen default rate; and α_{VaR} = quantile determined by the confidence level for *VaR*.

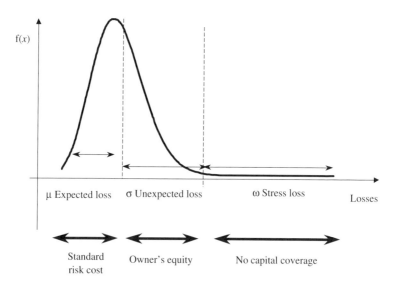

Figure 2.15	Coverage of operational risk

Although this concept is meant for the economic capital calculation on the financial institution's level, it can be used on a business-line level as well. Decomposition on a process level is even possible as long as the data basis can cope with it.

It is clear that the calculation concept underlies the same critical issues already mentioned for the statistical approaches. The value-at-risk concept allows the capital allocation to be based on past knowledge. New products, new business lines and new procedures unfortunately do not have a history and therefore it will be hard to calculate a value-at-risk amount. Furthermore, the capital allocation is affected not only by operational risk, and allocation for credit risk and market risk should also be included in the concept.

A Top-Down Approach for Capital Allocation

Hille, Burmeister and Otto (2000)[21] propose a top-down capital allocation based on the risk-adjusted return in the past. The measurement of the risk-adjusted return is based on the risk-adjusted performance measure (RAPM), which is calculated as follows:

$$\text{RAPM} = \frac{\text{income}}{\text{capital}} = \frac{\text{net income} - \text{expected losses} - \text{risk cost}}{\text{risk adjusted capital}}$$

The risk cost only includes the *unexpected risks* is this formula, since expected losses do not represent a risk according to the authors.

The risk capital per organizational unit for the period t is calculated as follows:

$$\text{Risk capital}_{org\ unit\ k}(t) = \text{RAPM}_{org\ unit\ k}(t-1) \times \lambda \times \text{total risk capital}$$

The shape factor λ is introduced, since the RAPM coefficients will not add up to 100 per cent.

Some issues should be considered while using this method:

• New business lines or products will not immediately bring positive or adequate results and therefore the RAPM will be low. If this issue is not noticed, the available risk capital in the next period will be automatically lower.

• If a business line performs with a negative RAPM, the model collapses in itself.

A solution for both issues has not been found yet, and they are to be noted while using the model in practice.

The Internal Risk Capital Market

Hille *et al.* (2000) alternatively propose to allocate the risk capital over the business lines by using an internal risk capital market. Contrary to the top-down approach, the method has a strong decentralized character. Moreover, the internal risk capital markets orient to the future need of risk capital per business line, whereas the top-down approach is focused on the risk capital need in the past. Each business line buys the risk capital needed on the internal risk capital market, and sells risk capital which is no longer bound by the business line's transactions or positions. Since risk capital can be bought and sold any time, the process is dynamic. The capital allocation is therefore not bound to a fixed period.

The use of this method requires a price for the risk capital held by the business lines, and the price is determined by the following parameters:

- The amount of risk capital held.
- The tenor of the risk capital transaction.
- The market price of risk capital.

The price is reflected as a rate per risk capital unit, and this rate should be valued as the expected risk-adjusted return. The Managing Board sets this expected risk-adjusted return rate based on the expectations of shareholders; the rate is therefore set equal to the required return on capital for the financial institution.

This method, however, leaves one problem to be solved: the risks of each business line are not independent; the position of one business line may be hedged by the position of another. The correlation coefficients for all business lines need to be calculated and should be considered if the required risk capital on a consolidated level for the financial institution is calculated. The risk for the financial institution on a consolidated level is:

$$R = \sqrt{\sum_{i,j} R_i \rho_{i,j} R_j}$$

where $\rho_{i,j}$ is the correlation coefficient between the risk position of business lines i and j. The financial institution will optimize the risk capital allocation in such a way that the usage of the available risk capital is maximized under consideration of the correlation effects. This scarce resource is therefore optimally allocated to each business line.

The idea of an internal risk capital market is valued positively since a more optimal allocation of risk capital is stimulated. Each business line has to pay for the risk capital taken and therefore risk capital which is no longer bound will be offered on the market. If the business line expands its business and therefore needs more risk capital, it need not fear that the risk capital offered to the internal market is lost. The business line offers the amount for a certain period to other business lines, and it is allowed to retract the 'contract' on the maturity date. In other allocation methods the business line often loses control over the risk capital which is not used any more, and this causes problems if the business line wants to grow at a later time. The business line will therefore react more politically and the financial institution will consequently miss possible transactions.

3 Management of Operational Risk

INTRODUCTION TO OPERATIONAL RISK MANAGEMENT

Operational risk management is motivated by at least the following factors:

- The regulatory capital charge,[1] which is about 20 per cent of the minimum capital charge of both credit and market risk under the old capital accord, is a substantial amount and should therefore be carefully managed. As soon as measurement methods[2] become more advanced and the regulators allow internal models, the management quality of operational risk will directly reflect the competitive position of the bank.
- Corporate governance[3] requires the management of corporates to introduce an adequate internal control framework, which should be embedded in a sound control environment. The managing board needs to explain the internal control framework and its adequacy in the financial statements, and the external auditor is required to review the statements of the managing board.
- The reputation loss caused by an operational risk affects the trust relationship between clients and the financial institution. The business relationship may be extraordinarily affected in the case of private banking, where private clients leave the management of their wealth in the hands of the account manager. Errors may disrupt this close relationship, even if the client's portfolio is not directly affected.
- Professional staff like to work in a professionally-oriented organization. If the financial organization is highly exposed to operational risk, relatively more errors will occur. More errors will not only damage the reputation of the financial institution; the reputation of the staff themselves will also be affected. It will become known that a lot of errors occurred in this house, which could affect staff's applications for jobs in other financial institutions – assessors will be aware of the reputation of the applicant's current employer. Therefore well-educated and experienced staff will resign as soon as they have the feeling that the financial institution's reputation is vulnerable; key staff will leave, and the financial institution is exposed to even more operational risk.

These points, besides the ethical rules, will motivate the financial institu-tion's management to manage operational risks in an adequate way. Such management, however, is economically bound as well; the expenses for risk-mitigating measures should not exceed the risk amount the financial institution is exposed to. The financial institution's management has four possibilities of action:

- Accept the operational risk
- Mitigate the operational risk
- Transfer operational risk
- Avoid operational risk

It is clear that management will make a trade-off between the expenses involved in the management decision and the risk the financial institution is exposed to. The first choice above is only valid in the case of calculated risk, where the consequences are controllable and the impact is normally low. Internal control measures to mitigate such risks may exceed the actual risk exposure involved.

The main part of this chapter is dedicated to the mitigation of opera-tional risk, which involves the following themes:

- The creation of a control environment;
- The introduction of knowledge management; and
- The use of the toolkit containing internal controls.

If mitigation of operational risk cannot be achieved, the transfer of opera-tional risk can be an alternative; through:

- Outsourcing of activities; or
- Insurance

Outsourcing should be accompanied by an adequate service-level agree-ment, since the financial institution is not allowed to fully delegate all responsibilities, having regard to the regulatory authorities. The liability of an outsourcing company is often limited to a certain amount, which may be inadequate to absorb the expected damage. The financial institution itself will outsource, since it perceives the risks involved as too high in comparison to expected earnings. Moreover, the financial institution is able to manage its expenses by keeping them variable instead of fixed.

Initiatives in the insurance market regarding operational risk will be discussed and the older insurance policies will also be described.

A final reaction may be to avoid the risk, which is equivalent to closing the business down. This option is only valid if the risks involved expose the financial institution in such a way that expected earnings cannot remain in any economically reasonable relationship to the risk exposure, and mitigation or transfer of operational risk is not an option.

Before the various management possibilities are discussed, the regulatory environment is considered, based on the German and Dutch regulations.

THE REGULATORY ENVIRONMENT

The regulatory environment still includes limited regulations regarding operational risk. At the time of writing (March 2001), both the Basle Committee and the European Commission have issued consultative documents, and additional quantitative studies are being conducted by the Basle Committee to estimate the effects of the proposed new capital accord. The new accord includes many changes regarding regulatory capital charges for credit risk, which have a huge impact on the calculation method and therefore on the regulatory capital required for credit risk. Just from a quantitative point of view, operational risk is a small document of only about 45 pages compared to the much larger credit risk section. The focus of management may be automatically directed to the credit risk issue, whereas an acute problem may be caused by the required regulatory capital charge for operational risk. The Basle Committee[4] expects that the regulatory capital charge under the old capital accord should be almost equal to the capital charge under the new capital accord *on an industry level*. The expectation, however, may be false at the micro level of the financial institution. The operational risk problem should therefore be given the attention it requires based on its impact on an organization, its competitive position and its commercial growth.

The existing regulations, however, do not offer much substance regarding operational risk. The German Banking Act[5] contains a paragraph regarding the management and control of financial institutions; some issues are touched in regulations of the regulatory authority (Bundesaufsichtsamt für das Kreditwesen), but no explicit regulations regarding operational risk exist at this moment. Operational risk themes are also scarce in other regulations in Europe. The Dutch central bank (DNB, 1988),[6] which acts as regulatory authority according to the Dutch Banking Act, published a memorandum regarding the reliability and continuity of IT systems in 1988; and in 1993 the Dutch central bank (DNB, 1993)[7] published a guideline regarding the organization of financial institutions.

The Basle Committee for Banking Supervision (Basle, 1998) published an internal-control framework for banks in 1998. This document should serve central banks in their supervisory role and is not compulsory for individual financial institutions; the document itself, however, is a good guide for individual financial institutions.

The regulations mentioned so far may be summarized as follows:

§25a of the German Banking Act (KWG): Organizational Duties of Institutions

The contents of paragraph 25a of the German Banking Act show the necessity for the regulatory authority to require organizational measures in financial institutions regarding the control of operational risk. The exact contents of this paragraph are:

Particular Organizational Duties of Institutions

An institution must:

1. have in place suitable arrangements for managing, monitoring and controlling risks and appropriate arrangements by means of which the institution's financial situation can be gauged with sufficient accuracy at all times;
2. have a proper business organization, an appropriate internal control system and adequate security precautions for the deployment of electronic data processing;
3. ensure that the records of executed business transactions permit full and unbroken supervision by the Federal Banking Supervisory Office for its area of responsibility; the requisite records shall be retained for six years; section 257 (3) and (5) of the Commercial Code applies as appropriate.

The outsourcing to another enterprise of operational areas that are essential for conducting banking business or providing financial services must impair neither the orderliness of such business or services nor the managers' ability to manage and monitor them, nor the Federal Banking Supervisory Office's right to audit and its ability to monitor them. In particular, the institution shall ensure by contractual means that it has the required powers to give instructions to the contractor in question and shall include the outsourced areas in its internal monitoring procedures. The institution shall report its intention to outsource operational areas, as well as the realization of its intention, to the Federal Banking Supervisory Office and the Deutsche Bundesbank immediately. The Federal Banking Supervisory Office forwards a copy of the report to the Federal Supervisory Office for Securities Trading.

This paragraph includes almost everything which should be arranged regarding the control of operational risk. Financial institutions are required to implement a process to manage and control the risks the organization is exposed to. The wording is such as to allow smaller financial institutions to comply with the law without investing in expensive IT systems. Small institutions sometimes have only small trading portfolios and the market risks involved can be represented without using dedicated market-risk control systems. For large financial institutions, however, it can hardly be imagined that they could control their risks without using a group-wide control concept; for them, credit risks and market risks cannot be properly represented without the use of IT systems.

The management and control of operational risks, however, is not included in current theories and practice regarding bank controls, although the legal requirement can be derived from §25a.

The legal requirement is not limited to the management and control of risks. The organization should be balanced in regard to the risks to which it is exposed. The organization should include an internal control framework supported by security measures in the IT environment of the bank. If this requirement is broadly interpreted, then both prevention and damage-control measures are included. The IT environment is especially mentioned since financial institutions are highly dependent on their systems. The regulatory institutions are not only responsible for each single institute, but also for the stability of the financial system in a country as a whole. If the payment system in a country collapses, the economy may fall into chaos and even the country's social stability may be endangered. In the payment area in particular, financial institutions are almost completely dependent on their IT systems. It is not without reason that the Dutch central bank issued a memorandum on the reliability and continuity of IT systems.

A financial institution's organization should allow the regulatory authority to check all transactions completely. The complete recording of transactions should therefore be guaranteed by a sound internal control framework. Measures like segregation of duties between the front office and the back office and a procedure to control the complete matching of confirmations need to be implemented in order to document compliance with regulatory requirements.

Many financial institutions have outsourced parts of their business. In such situations the regulatory authority needs to ensure that the responsibility for the management and control of outsourced activities and the supervisory audit possibilities have not become limited. The managing board of the financial institution is therefore liable for the activities of third parties against the regulatory authorities in the case of outsourcing. The service-level agreement should allow the management of the financial institution to instruct the third party, and the supervisory function of the regulatory authority should be explicitly declared in this document. At this moment (March 2001), the new guideline regarding outsourcing is under discussion by the supervisor.

The Dutch Central Bank Memorandum, 1988

The Dutch central bank stressed the importance of IT systems for an error-free processing of banking transactions in its Memorandum of 1988. The Dutch supervisor requires financial institutions to minimize the drivers which negatively influence the solvency and liquidity of these institutions. The central bank mainly focuses on payment services, since a disruption in this area could destabilize the economic system.

The central bank formulated the reliability and continuity of IT systems as criteria and imposed requirements regarding the internal control framework within a financial institution. A focus was laid on the general, application and users' controls in and around IT systems. Even non-voting members of the board of directors should inform themselves about the activities of the bank regarding the mentioned controls, and advise on improvements if necessary. The board of directors should base its assessment on the audit notes of the external auditor, who is required to inform the central bank about the quality of the new implemented measures.

The Dutch Central Bank Guideline Regarding the Internal Organization of Financial Institutions

The Dutch central bank issued a guideline regarding the requirements of organization of financial institutions in 1993. The guideline was also a reaction to the Barings Bank problem. The main content was the explanation of the importance of a functioning internal control system and the responsibility of the board of directors for the financial institution's organization. The appendix to the guideline contains many practical examples, but they are not compulsory for each institution.

Apart from the regulatory capital charge the financial institution has other reasons to manage operational risk. In the next section the measures to mitigate operational risk are described.

THE TOOLKIT[8]

Introduction to the Use of the Toolkit

The toolkit is a collection of internal control measures which mitigate the operational risks. The implementation of internal controls underlies the contingency principle: each individual situation needs its own assessment and as a result a specific set of internal control measures. In this chapter each such measure will be discussed including its effect, in some cases with examples.

It should also be considered that the implementation of internal control measures costs money, and such measures should therefore stay within a reasonable relationship to the expected damages in case of non-mitigated operational risks.

The Contents of the Toolkit

The toolkit contains the following components:

- Policies and procedures
- Segregation of duties
- Dual control
- Proxy instruction
- Confirmations
- Reconciliations
- Plausibility checks
- Determination and control of counterparty and trading limits
- Inventory check
- Implementation of an independent internal control function
- Control measures to guarantee error-free IT processing
- Recruitment of reliable personnel

These tools can be used as components to build procedures. For example the segregation of duties will be found in almost all procedures in a financial institution.

However, these tools will only function correctly if the control environment in which they are embedded is properly established. Also, as well as the control environment, a well-implemented knowledge-management system is of the greatest importance in order to mitigate operational risk properly. Both the control environment and the role of knowledge management will be discussed before moving on to the components of the toolkit.

The Implementation of a Control Environment

The implementation of a control environment starts with control awareness. All management levels should acknowledge the importance of internal control measures and implement them effectively. They should be implemented in the right intensity and quantity, and only such measures as are appropriate to each situation should be chosen from the toolkit.

The desired results are formulated as targets in a functioning control environment, and the achievement of these targets will be checked on a regular basis. These checks should be performed not only at the operational level, they need to be implemented on both the tactical and strategic levels as well. The implementation on all management levels will improve transparency in the financial institution, since it is clear that everybody takes responsibility for the duties delegated. Senior management should seriously check their own achievements as well, since this will be a clear signal in the organization that the same rules are valid for everyone.

The comparison between budget and actual figures should not be the end of the procedure. Responsible staff members and managers should consider which measures can be taken to improve the current situation. The proposed actions, which are collected in an action plan, should include due dates, which are then checked by the control function to ensure they are met on a regular basis.

The implementation of a risk management function and especially the installation of counterparty and trading limits belong to the control environment. If management does not react when limits are exceeded, nobody should be surprised if traders do not see a limit excess as a serious problem. The financial institution may be exposed to huge risks if the control environment is not well-established, and if a limit excess occurs, management should be immediately informed by the trader. Dependent on the amount of the excess, the board member responsible for trading should also be informed, since this board member should approve excesses. A limit excess approval should contain the excess amount and the expected tenor of the excess. If the excess is approved, the timely resolution should be checked.

A well-developed control environment is also expressed by the installation of a new business committee. This committee reviews each new product or product variant proposal on the ability to process the described product in compliance with the policies of the financial institution and the regulatory requirements. Not only the limit control process in the trading activity of the financial institution or the processing in the back office are affected, but also the representation of the new product or product variant in the regulatory reporting process. If the bank's regulatory reporting contains errors, the financial institution's reputation is also endangered. The regulatory capital position of the financial institution may even be wrongly calculated due to a false classification of the product, which may lead to opportunity costs for the financial institution. The unnecessarily allocated capital could have been used for other transactions, which could have contributed to the results of the financial institution.

The new business committee should ensure that all participants have the same level of necessary knowledge about the new product and its features. A new product sometimes has unknown features; and sometimes a combination of two existing products may lead to another mix of features than just their individual features. Also, the risks of one product may be compensated by the features of the other, which causes another risk profile of the product. The new risk profile should be exactly determined by the new business committee, especially for risk management purposes.

The processing of a structured product within the investment banking activity may play an important role in the new business committee as well. The new committee should determine exactly which settlements need to be executed. In some cases the cash flows of a structural product need to be executed in various marketplaces, each with its own settlement conventions. The back office is confronted with the task of settling all parts of the transaction in such a way that the cash flow is not interrupted. Structured products are mostly designed so that the cash flows of all the basis products under consideration fall within a profit margin hedge. In most cases the cash flows are large amounts; if they cannot be matched, the financial institution has to fund for the missing cash flow. In this case the damage caused by this operational risk is the interest, which needs to be paid for the funding transaction. Moreover, a reputational loss may be the case since the counterparties are mostly professional investors who require a top service from the financial institution. Since structured products are mostly responsible for high profit margins, the loss of the client may cause an income loss of millions of euros.

The new business committee will certainly not only be installed to offer the right information to risk manager, controller and settlement departments, it also plays an important role for the front office. The front office should know which structured products, under which conditions, can be processed in the financial institution. If the front office would like to offer a structured product which includes both home and foreign products, both the front office and the back office need to be familiar with the settlement conventions of the respective markets.

The control environment does not simply come into existence through being described in the organization's manual. The necessary organizational structures not only belong to the control environment, they are an important prerequisite for it. Another important prerequisite is the behaviour of senior management: managers should show that they are aware of the impact of a functioning control environment and they should be good examples for their personnel. If managers do not take the internal control measures seriously themselves, they should not expect that other staff members will adhere to these measures. The 'tone at the top' should align with the expected behaviour of the financial institution's employees. The building of a control environment therefore starts at the top of the financial institution.

Transparency is an important result of the establishment of an effective control environment, and should be considered before it is introduced to the financial institution. Individual contributions to the institution's results become known, which may reveal some unbalanced situations. Senior management may avoid conflicts and reduce fears among managers by creating a clear transparency around their own activities. If the managers see that senior management takes the issue seriously, they will more quickly adopt the controls and transparency procedures themselves.

As soon as the control environment has been established, the other measures of the toolkit will be more effective. The increased effectiveness is expressed in more certainty that the internal control measures will be executed and that management will react on time to alarm signals, if any.

Knowledge Management

Knowledge management is not well-established within financial institutions. In the past the necessity has not been so urgent, since most staff members were employed by financial institutions for many years; job-hopping was not a common practice in those days. Such stability may be still true for smaller savings and co-operative banks, but with larger banks the situation has dramatically changed. Discussions about possible mergers may also negatively affect the stability of human resources. Well-experienced and educated staff will generally not have a 'wait-and-see' attitude in the case of a threatening merger; they will look for other opportunities in the labour market. Such staff members, however, are important for the success of the financial institution since they carry a large knowledge value with them. Other employees with less-promising chances on the labour market are forced to stay with the bank. This problem is called adverse selection; it is clear that resignations of knowledgeable staff exposes the financial institution to a large operational risk.

Another situation may be observed with small banks or foreign branches of internationally operating financial institutions. The number of employees in such institutions is not that large, and therefore many responsibilities are concentrated on just a few staff members. Such employees are able to cover a broad range of all tasks to be performed, and they are therefore quite attractive on the labour market. They may easily find another job if their current job becomes uncertain, or if they perceive their current situation as uncertain. Foreign branches of internationally operating financial institutions are particularly under constant cost pressures. Improvements in processing are continuously considered in order to save costs, and in Europe a centralization tendency can be observed, especially in the European Union. Trading activities are often concentrated in one location in Europe (in many cases in London), and in some cases corporate centre functions are concentrated as well. It is clear that such measures may lead to unrest in companies, which may finally result in the resignation of experienced staff.

The banking business has become more knowledge-intensive in recent years, and corporate financial products are good examples. Knowledge from many other disciplines is necessary to make the product successful, for example tax expertise, accounting knowledge, international law and financial engineering knowledge. The financial institution needs to transform knowledge, in addition to the classical transformation roles of scale, risk and tenor. This transformation requires a well-functioning knowledge-management system, since a new product is only successful if the financial institution is able to combine the knowledge of all the various types of staff members. If this knowledge is concentrated among only one or a few staff members, the loss of those employees may result in discontinuity of a complete, or part of a, business line.

It is not only knowledge about processes and products which may be lost due to resignations. The financial institution may also lose knowledge about actual or potential customers, since client contacts are mostly based on personal relationships. If a relationship manager leaves, he normally takes most of his knowledge with him. Many financial institutions still do not use systems in which knowledge about customers is systematically recorded. The loss involved in lost customer contacts may be easily quantified: it is the present value of the future income which could have been generated out of these relationships.

In these cases knowledge management is a prerequisite to protect the organization from such losses. Another critical factor is the knowledge about alternative processing possibilities if the normal processing flow cannot be followed. This knowledge needs to be immediately available if an incident occurs. The conservation of this type of knowledge is not easy, since many employees have difficulties in documenting their knowledge.

These difficulties may be caused by different triggers:

- The employee knows that knowledge implies power;
- The employee considers some process steps as common sense and therefore forgets to document them; or
- The employee thinks that the knowledge is familiar to other colleagues and therefore does not document it.

In the first case the bank is confronted with a difficult situation; the employee may not want to disclose his knowledge since he knows that nothing functions without his input. Such conduct may be triggered if the employee thinks that his job may be endangered, when he may even try to hide his knowledge from others in order to make himself irreplaceable. As soon as this employee resigns, the financial institution is heavily affected and the consequences of this lack of knowledge will be perceivable for quite some time.

Regarding the second point, if an employee executes his repetitive tasks on a daily basis, then most necessary knowledge becomes familiar and easy to him. If one of his colleagues has to perform the job, many things may turn out to be not as simple as the jobholder thought. Even existing documentation may be of little help to colleagues, since the simple tasks have not been documented; and often when tasks are delegated to colleagues only special issues are discussed. Problems may occur not only if an employee resigns or goes on holiday; in the case of illness, the employee may not be able to hand over his tasks properly to colleagues and therefore the probability of errors may significantly increase.

The third case is more dangerous to a financial institution. Employees often assume that colleagues know about their tasks and responsibilities, and of course colleagues may know many details about the job of a specific employee, since they are working in a team. However, colleagues may never have performed the tasks themselves and will therefore not be up to date regarding the details which need to be considered when the tasks are actually performed. If the colleagues discuss the tasks with the employee concerned, the impression may be given that the colleagues know exactly what should be done in each detailed step of the process; and the employee may rely on his colleagues and expect that his tasks are performed exactly during his absence. Reality shows another picture in most cases: colleagues perform the tasks in conformity to their existing knowledge and the errors made are discovered at a later stage. Correction may be too late, since damage for the bank already exists.

An adequate knowledge-management strategy should not only solve the above-mentioned problems, it should also enable the financial institution to structure the available knowledge in order to guarantee the institution's renewal and innovation potential. Thomas Stewart (1997) calls this knowledge capital, three sources of which are:

- Human knowledge
- Structured knowledge in the organization
- Customer knowledge

Structured knowledge is considered as standardized approaches, manuals, instructions and other media which are used to document knowledge. Management should transform tacit human knowledge and customer knowledge into structured knowledge. Knowledge which exists at many places, but which is not retrievable, should be documented and published within the financial institution, in order that the knowledge capital of the institution can be safeguarded by this transformation. This is illustrated in Figure 3.1.

But how is this to be done? There are several possible answers. First, employees' knowledge should be shared by other employees. Management could request employees to document their knowledge, but this request is likely to be unsuccessful; many employees may have difficulties in documenting their tasks as described above. Moreover, documentation is seen as a low-level task, since it does not benefit the professional in the short term. Therefore management should take other measures. Knowledge may be shared in informal groups in which staff members meet each other since they are personally interested in the activities of their colleagues. The effect is that the shared knowledge is owned by the group, although no member of this group owns the knowledge exclusively. Stewart[9] calls these groups 'communities of practice'. Most employees belong to communities of practice; these communities may focus on both the professional and the private sides of life.

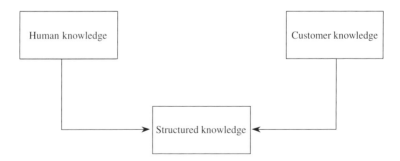

Figure 3.1 The transformation of important knowledge in structured knowledge

Senior management should not manage these groups conventionally; if conventional management was tried, the group as such could be destroyed. Management should simply stimulate these groups and establish the right conditions in order to make them successful in the financial institution.

The conclusion should not be drawn that traditional methods of knowledge management are obsolete. Especially in the more standardized areas of the financial institution, much knowledge may be structured in procedures and working instructions. These often help to improve the quality of products which are processed through these procedures.

Also, customer knowledge can be transformed into structured knowledge. In Figure 3.2, *customer profitability* has a central position in the structured customer information. All connected areas in the figure determine customer profitability directly or indirectly. *Customer needs* are a key success factor. Only the financial institution which is able to correctly understand these needs and satisfy them has a chance to engage in a long-lasting relationship with the customer. The following themes belong in the customer needs information:

- What is the strategy of the customer?
- With which burning problems is the customer currently confronted?
- Which changes in law and regulations (civil law, tax law) affect the customer's business?
- In what ways does the customer control his national and international liquidity flows?

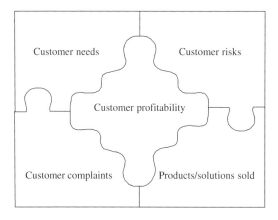

Figure 3.2 Customer information

The *customer risks* for the financial institution are twofold:

- Default risk
- Performance risk

The default risk is probably the oldest risk the financial institution is exposed to. A good overview of the default parameter is not only important for the control of the default risk, but also for the pricing of the credit-risk-related products of the financial institution. In the end the creditability of the customer determines the credit spread in the interest rates.

The performance risk is manifest in the case of a guarantee. If the customer (e.g. a construction firm) promises his client that the airport can use a new runway at a specified date and the client (the airport) requires a performance bond (which is a guarantee), the financial institution is held to pay under the guarantee as soon as the default situation as described in the bond is manifest. At that moment the financial institution is exposed to a credit risk regarding its customer. If the financial institution did not decrease the customer's limit by the amount of the guarantee, the financial institution could be confronted with difficulties during the collection of the claim. Although this risk is in itself a credit risk, it is often treated separately since the cause is different.

Customer complaints are mostly unpleasant since they can be the start of a disturbance of the trust relationship between the customer and the financial institution. It is therefore important to systematically record all customer complaints, so that all staff members know what complaints exist (so that the causes should not repeat with other customers) and what measures were taken to solve the problem. It is interesting to know if the complaint was used as an opportunity to talk with the customer about his needs. Moreover, the relationship manager should know if open customer complaints exist before he calls a customer. If the relationship manager is not informed, the customer may be irritated and feel that his complaint has not been taken seriously. If the financial institution uses a call centre, a structured customer complaint system is extremely important since a personal relationship between the customer and the staff member in the call centre does not exist.

The *products and solutions sold* are not just a performance indicator for the relationship manager, but they also form an indication of how intensively the relationship is managed. Cross-selling ratios show whether an intensive relationship management has been successful. An analysis of the ratio may even open up new market potential if existing relationships can be intensified or successful solutions with other customers can be repeated.

If knowledge management is successfully implemented in a financial organization, the effects of a high staff turnover rate may be significantly decreased. Knowledge management is therefore also an important damage control tool for the financial institution.

Policies and Procedures

Policies are general guidelines decided by the board of directors, describing how the financial institution covers certain areas of interest. A policy which arranges the description of procedures is available in most organizations. The minimum requirements of procedures are formulated, the methods and tools used for the design of procedures are explained and their form is made clear. The following policies are quite common within financial institutions:

- A remuneration policy.
- An appraisal policy.
- An IT policy (which defines the hardware and software used in the financial institution).
- A treasury policy (which products are traded, which limits are defined and controlled, which responsibilities are given).
- An internal audit policy (mandate of the internal audit department, the audit tools used) in which the independence and neutrality of the internal audit department is made clear.
- The implementation of external regulations is often arranged by a policy; for example a compliance policy and a money-laundering policy.

Policies are the basis for the design of procedures.

Procedures describe the way products or information are processed by the various functions; some examples are:

- A procedure for trading, processing and settlement of interest-rate derivatives.
- A procedure for the drafting of management information.

The other tools are components which will be used within the procedures design.

Segregation of Duties

Segregation of duties is based on the old principle of specialization. If employees separately specialize in certain activities, they may achieve better results together than if they handle all tasks themselves.

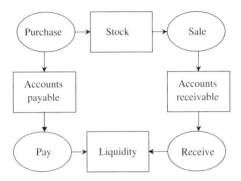

Figure 3.3   Value chain of a trading organization

The segregation of duties can be easily explained along the value chain of an organization. The simplest form is the value chain of a normal trading company, as shown in Figure 3.3. The ellipses represent the various activities, the boxes show the assets and liabilities of the company. It is clear that if the purchase and sales functions are combined with one staff member, the integrity of all revenues cannot be guaranteed since this staff member is able to sell without involving the company at all. Ergo, the gross revenues will not be reflected in the company's profit and loss account, but on the bank account of the employee.

Segregation of duties is based on contradictory interests of employees. The procurement head will not be interested to register less purchases than he really bought, and the storage department has no interest to register more inventory than really available. The recording function is able to match the following relationship:

$$\text{Inventory}_{\text{start of period}} + \text{Purchase} - \text{Sales} = \text{Inventory}_{\text{end of period}}$$

In a financial institution, however, it is hard to differentiate between money flows and material flows. 'Material flows' in a bank are also money flows at the same time. Nevertheless, segregation of duties is also important in financial institutions and the following segregations can be identified:

- Authorization
- Safeguarding
- Recording
- Execution

These functions should always be segregated in an ideal situation. Well-known segregations of duties are:

- Front office versus back office;
- Back office /front office versus accounting and controlling; and
- Static data maintenance versus transaction processing.

In each situation in which the completeness and accuracy of business data cannot be guaranteed, the implementation of segregation of duties is valid.

Dual Control

Dual control is often seen as equal to segregation of duties, although an important difference exists. Dual control means that two employees contribute to the performance of one task. Especially in cases where segregation of duties is not effective as when contradictory interests between staff members do not exist, dual control can be an effective tool to mitigate operational risk. The following implementations of dual control are well-known:

- The data-entry and verification function in the case of transaction processing;
- The instruction that all documentation, which obliges the financial institution legally, needs to be signed by two authorized staff members.

The verification function can be implemented in two different ways:

- The employee verifies the entered data on sight and confirms their correctness; or
- The employee has to re-key certain data and the system compares the re-keyed data with the original keyed data. If a match is recognized, the transaction is accepted.

It need not be argued that the last method is the more secure, although this procedure is more expensive. It should therefore be carefully considered in which cases the method is to be implemented.

The implementation of a verification function should be considered in the case of static data as well, since the consequences of errors in such data can have an exponential effect in comparison to errors in transaction processing. For example, if the account number in a standing settlement instruction is wrongly entered in the system, all cash flows will be routed in a wrong direction and the financial institution is liable for all interest claims which may arise as a consequence of this error. The errors may also affect the reputation of the financial institution. If the name of a new customer is spelt incorrectly, the customer may feel irritated and not taken seriously by the financial institution. A wrong address may lead to correspondence between the bank and the customer becoming known by third parties, which will directly affect the trust relationship between the customer and the financial institution. Not only the customer may be lost, but also opportunity losses may exist since the customer may discuss this issue with friends and in other business relationships.

Proxy Instruction

The proxy instruction describes the limitation of authority of staff members. Both activities and amounts can be limited; for example in many cases the sale of fixed assets is limited to the board of directors. The authorities are normally classified in various classes, which describe the amounts and the activities to which the holder of the authority is entitled. In many cases the amounts and activities increase if two staff members with authorities out of different classes sign off both for the same activity.

Since many tasks are performed by electronically supported systems today, a special issue is seen in the maintenance of the proxy instruction in these systems. Especially in the case of workflow systems, the transaction can be processed automatically and unauthorized payments may be executed without involvement of the staff members with the right authorities. Nevertheless employees should be adequately empowered in order to perform their jobs. A trade off between strict controls on the one hand, and efficient operating on the other, needs to be considered.

Confirmations

In the case of financial institutions where the segregation of duties may not be so effective as in a trading company, it is particularly important to involve third parties in the internal control process. The confirmation plays an important role in the case of financial derivatives, since the first on-balance effects may occur after a couple of months. In the case of an interest-rate swap the first interest payment is, for example, due after six months. If the transaction is not properly processed, the financial institution bases its decisions on incorrect interest-position information. Such errors can be avoided if the transactions are confirmed by third parties (in this case by the counterparties). In the case of financial derivatives it is common that both counterparties send each other a confirmation, which also represents the cash flows related to the traded product in detail. Both parties will check the confirmation of the counterparty carefully and sign the document as soon as the representation of the trade matches with its representation in the financial institution's systems. The matching of confirmations and the checking of these documents should be formalized in a procedure.

A particular issue is the problem of failing confirmations, which may have different causes. The counterparty probably did not receive the confirmation, for example. Or the confirmation may have been lost in the counterparty's organization. In the worst case the financial institution is confronted with a fraud case: the transaction turns out to be vague, the trader has introduced the vague transaction to avoid heavy swings in the profit and loss account or to prevent a limit breach. The financial institution should therefore have a clear process for handling missing confirmations. The settlements manager should check the open confirmations on a regular basis, and senior management should be informed as soon as an accepted confirmation fails. Senior management should involve the internal audit department as well, in order to check if the transaction has been properly executed and processed. The internal audit department may in turn correspond with the counterparty's audit department as well in order to clarify reasons for missing confirmations. If the accepted confirmation fails after all possible efforts, senior management should consider cancelling the relationship with the counterparty.

Reconciliations

Reconciliations between independent registrations are very important in financial institutions to minimize operational risk. The critical steps in the processes involved are checked in detail, and reconciliations should guarantee the completeness and accuracy of the transaction processing. Securities processing is taken as an example in this case as shown in Figure 3.4.

The bank needs to state whether all closed transactions are really processed and settled. Moreover, the securities themselves need to be delivered in the case of a buy, or in the case of a sale the money flow should be received (which is normally booked in the account with the central bank). In order to check the completeness and accuracy of data flows, the following positions are reconciled:

- Front-office position = back-office position. The reconciliation guarantees that the same transactions are processed in both systems.
- Back-office position = balance of the securities accounts in the general ledger (in this case proprietary trading is assumed).

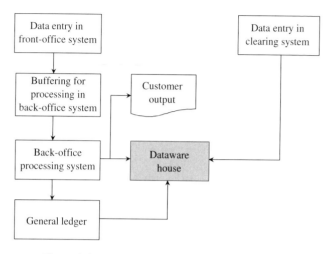

Figure 3.4   Data flows in the security order process

- Sum of buys of a certain security as represented in the back-office system – the sum of the sales of this security = sum of the security in the delivery list of the clearing house and the delivery date. In most cases the reconciliation can be performed per trade since the details are offered per trade as well.
- The money outflow representing the security buys – money inflow representing the sales = money outflow regarding security trading in the account with the central bank.

The reconciliations may be easily understandable at first glance. It should be noted that delivery of securities is executed two days after the trade date; and different value dates of the posted item may need some extra attention as well. If all data flow together in a database, the financial institution may be able to reconcile a high percentage of trades automatically, which may relieve the departments involved. The freed time can then be used for other more value-adding tasks.

It should be noted that the above illustration has been simplified; in practice many special details need to be considered. For example if a financial institution uses brokers to execute trades, it may happen that one transaction is sliced into ten pieces by the broker, which will make the reconciliation more difficult.

Reconciliation of suspense accounts should be executed on a regular basis (at least monthly to allocate open items to the correct balance sheet lines). These accounts play an important role in the processing activities of a financial institution, but they are a considerable source of errors at the same time. At the end of each period the balance on the account should be exactly specified out of the single open items. The controller will check whether 'refreshment' of old open items has been performed; refreshment means posting old open items to other suspense accounts to give them a 'fresh' booking date to avoid nasty questions from the internal audit department and controller.

In all cases where system borderlines are passed or segregation of duties has been implemented, a reconciliation should be considered. Automated reconciliations will not only be more efficient, they will also enable timely execution. If time passes, losses may increase exponentially and investigation is more difficult.

Plausibility Checks

Plausibility checks should be conducted to check the validity of data processing; although it should be noted that 100 per cent accuracy cannot be guaranteed. The following examples can be mentioned:

- New closed deals in a month $\times$ average interest rate $\times$ time = increase in interest income in the profit and loss account.
- Repayments $\times$ original interest rates $\times$ time = decrease in interest income in the profit and loss account.
- The daily booked income should only differ by about 5000 euros at most from yesterday's amount. Higher differences should be investigated.
- Transaction volume of payment orders $\times$ average fee = sum of the booked fees in a period.

Other examples may be formulated in the same way. Many plausibility checks can be automated and give both management and controllers a good insight if the supplied numbers are reliable.

Determination and Control of Counterparty and Trading Limits

Limits are normally used to control credit and market risks. At the same time such limits may prevent incorrect data entry (it is assumed that the limit check is performed immediately after the data entry). If a typographic error occurs (such as a zero too many), the probability may be high that the limit check will stop the transaction due to a limit breach.

Another error that can easily occur is in the entry of an option transaction, which is used for hedging cash instruments. If the same number of option contracts is ordered as the number of cash instruments to be hedged, the hedge can be factor 100 too high (since one option contract represents 100 cash instruments); a trading limit check may prevent such an error.

Inventory Check

An internal control measure which should not fail is to check for a match between account balances and real available assets such as cash, securities and also the balances in the nostro accounts of the financial institution. These checks should be executed on a regular basis, and at least at the end of the year the external auditor will take a sample to be counted in detail to audit whether the numbers are satisfactory. The inventory checks should be performed by staff independent of the staff members responsible for the storage of these assets, and these controls should be performed randomly to ensure that the responsible staff are not tempted to 'tidy up' the figures.

It is important that the time delay between retrieving the balance of the corresponding account and the inventory check itself is kept to a minimum. Otherwise the staff responsible for the storage may inform the accounting department and the balance may be adjusted to the amount counted during the inventory check. The check would then result in a satisfactory outcome, even though a mismatch had just been hidden.

Implementation of an Independent Internal Control Function

Although the independent internal audit function is required by most supervisors in almost all countries, it should play an important role in a financial institution's activities quite apart from this statutory requirement. Since it is quite difficult to follow sophisticated modern products, senior management should be able to rely on the proper functioning of internal controls and efficient internal organization. Reliability should be verified by internal audits conducted according to a risk-oriented audit plan.

The internal auditors plan their audits based on the risks involved in the various processes, and the possible effects of errors. The audit frequency of, for example, the equity derivatives trading desk would therefore be higher than the audit frequency of the mailroom. The independence of the internal audit department is expressed in the department's position: the head of the internal audit department normally reports directly to the chief executive officer. In many Anglo-Saxon countries the head of the internal audit department even reports directly to the chairman of the board of directors.

On behalf of senior management, the internal audit department checks that all procedures are adhered to and that the financial institution is not therefore extraordinarily exposed to operational risk. The importance of the internal auditor's role increases if the auditors are willing to consult management regarding improvements as well. However, consulting by auditors is sometimes under dispute; some auditors have the opinion that consultation conflicts with the internal audit role. If the auditor advises incorrectly, he may feel himself in an impossible position to present negative audit findings in the next audit. Managers may even misuse the situation by involving auditors at an early stage in order to protect themselves from negative audit findings in the future.

However, it would be unfortunate if all internal auditors were unwilling to consult the business line partners regarding risks involved and possible ways to mitigate these risks. Auditors are normally quite experienced in the use of internal controls and know very well the boundaries of these controls. The boundaries of internal controls are especially interesting in the design phase of a process, and may be overlooked since the focus of the design staff involved is elsewhere. The role of the internal auditor should therefore be very clear to all staff members. If the auditor advises on internal controls for a new process, the other parties should note his position and leave him room to audit the process after implementation as well. This issue can also be addressed in the internal policy.

The internal audit department reports the operational risks as audit findings to management and may also recommend solutions to the audit findings. The solutions may be derived from discussions between auditor and auditee. Senior management is then responsible for controlling the implementation of the improvements as proposed in the internal audit report.

Control Measures to Guarantee Error-free IT Processing

The controls in the IT environment are often classified as follows:

- General controls
- Application controls
- User controls

The general controls have already been discussed in detail. Summarizing, the following controls can be mentioned:

- Physical access control to the hardware
- Logical access to the systems

- Change management
- Capacity management
- Emergency planning
- Backup recovery procedures

Capacity management becomes more and more important in transaction banking. The availability control regarding systems, networks and data storage capacity is essential; if systems are not available the bank may be liable to customers and compensation payments may need to be made for damages caused by failures to trade. Moreover, network experts are hard to hire due to the labour market situation and the pressured margins of direct banks.

A continuous availability control can only be achieved if control software is used. The software checks whether active components such as router, hubs and switches are available, but also the availability of the server is controlled. The system also checks that internal memory and data storage capacity is not reaching predefined limits. Network traffic is also controlled, in order to avoid data traffic jams. The network manager can decide to reroute a part of the data traffic, or sometimes data transmission may be stopped to avoid disturbing other more important transmissions. The network manager therefore needs to prioritize according to the relative importance of each data transmission. A data transmission regarding payment services is more important than a data transmission for the management information system; the latter also contains a great deal of data and therefore uses a lot of bandwidth.

The control is not bound to any particular location; it is possible to control remotely. Network management can be centralized and some large banks have concentrated their network control in three locations to cover all time zones. Figure 3.5 illustrates a typical network control system. In the figure, a WAN (Worldwide Area Network) is shown. In the middle are two routers which enable connection between the mission-critical system and one of

Figure 3.5 Mission-critical system

the foreign branches of the financial institution. Since this infrastructure is used for trading purposes, single point failures must be avoided as much as possible. Therefore two encryptors are used, as shown at the right side of the picture. The mission-critical system controls continuously if one of the encryptors is available. The routers, which are finally responsible for the connection within the WAN, are controlled by a high standby router protocol which controls continuously if one of the routers is available. The system is so configured that it is able to find alternative ways to guarantee proper data transmission. The system will also inform the network administrator as soon as the primary connection fails, since a failure in the secondary connection would have serious consequences as a backup would not be available at that moment.

Both routers and switches are controlled by the network performance control software. Boxes in the system display show green if all parameters are below the critical values; if they become red, critical values have been exceeded. Traffic through a router is monitored continuously; peak values are recorded for both the transmitted frames and transmitted bits, and these values are shown graphically in Figure 3.6.

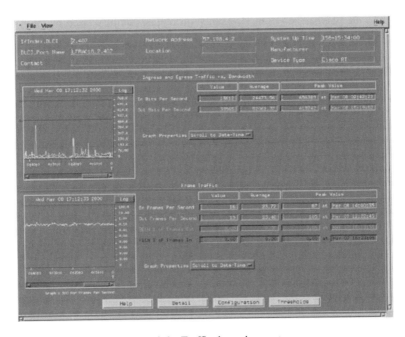

Figure 3.6   Traffic through a router

From Figure 3.6 it can be seen that the performance of this router was not in a critical phase. In the upper graph two lines can be seen which represent a warning and a critical level. The network administrator will also receive a warning if the data transmission is affected, at which point he is able to take corrective measures.

The application controls should check for complete and accurate processing by the application, for example by:

- Reconciliations;
- Hash totals (e.g. a summation of account number × balance amounts, checked between the source and receiving systems to prove the completeness and accuracy of an interface between the two IT systems; or
- Reference checks (e.g. does the customer exist, which customer number was included in a transaction data entry?).

Reconciliations are not just performed to check the completeness of data in a database; they may be used to prove the completeness of a calculation as well. Especially in the case of new products introduced after the initial date of installation of an application, controls need to be implemented. If these products are not represented in the reports, the information is incomplete and may cause wrong decisions. Problems may be caused by the following issues:

- The new product is not recognized by the management information system; or
- The product is recognized by the management information system, but it is not included in the selection for the report.

In the first case the management information system does not see the new product. The product has a product-id which is not included in the system and therefore the product is not accepted by this system. The handling of the corresponding records depends on the error-handling measures which are implemented in the management information system. In the worst case the records are rejected without any notice, and nobody will even recognize that the database is incomplete. In some cases the mentioned records will be temporarily stored in a separate table, and the data administrator is informed by the system. Experts should then check why these records are not processed correctly, and take corrective actions; the records are then offered again for processing to the management information system. If records are stored in the error table, it is advisable to print a warning text on the report which indicates that the information is possibly incomplete or inaccurate. This action may prevent decision-makers from taking wrong decisions based on the information presented.

If an error-handling procedure is not defined properly and the records are just inserted in the database, the reports are not automatically complete. Reports are normally based on an SQL-statement (Standard Query Language), in which the product-ids are included as selection criteria. The query may therefore simply pass the records which include a product-id, even though they may not satisfy other selection criteria. The created information is therefore incomplete and it may be expected that this problem is not noticed.

Reconciliations are the key to avoid such difficulties. These reconciliations do not just include the matching of the number of records in the source system and the receiving system, but also the reconciliation of financial data. Figure 3.7 illustrates a possible reconciliation process.

The following issues should be considered in the case of reconciliations:

- The records of reversed transactions should not be considered during the reconciliation;
- The reconciliation should be performed per currency; and
- The reconciliation should be adjusted to the general ledger accounts scheme.

If this reconciliation is consequently performed for all products, the risk of incomplete recording is greatly minimized. However, the risk of a movement of data between records (e.g. the current value of lending contract 1

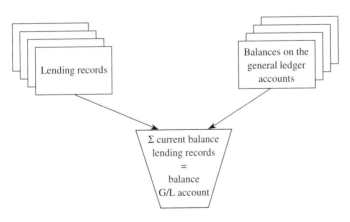

Figure 3.7 Reconciliation of financial data

is represented in the record of lending contract 2, and vice versa) is not excluded by this control. If the balances on the general ledger accounts separated in debit and credit amounts are added and matched with the balance sheet total, a cross system reconciliation will exist which guarantees the completeness and accuracy of the data.

It is highly recommended that the results of reconciliations are given in the reports. The user of the information can then ensure himself that the information meets his quality requirements.

Hash totals are a special form of reconciliation. A hash total is an addition of single non-homogeneous figures, whose sum is often used to prove the accuracy and completeness of the data transmission between various systems. Hash totals are normally calculated per row to exclude the risk of a movement of data. A possible form may be the multiplication of balance and account numbers with the results added. The calculation is performed in both the source system and the receiving system and the results are compared. If a match is found, it is almost certain that the data transmission was error-free.

Reference checks are especially performed in the case of a database management system, and should guarantee the integrity of the database. If a customer data record is going to be deleted and the database still contains transactions which were concluded with this customer, a reference check should avoid the deletion of the customer record. Otherwise the transaction records will 'ghost' in the database and calculation modules will not recognize these records anymore.

Unexpected situations should also be anticipated in the case of application control development; the following examples can be mentioned:

• A lending amount can only be released if a counterparty limit has been entered in the system.
• In the case of a limit excess an approval is necessary before processing the affected transaction.
• Before accounting entries are processed, the system will check if the account numbers to be used are really available.
• If accounts are closed, it should be checked in advance if (standing) orders still exist which need to be processed.

User controls are human controls, which should check the complete and accurate processing by systems. The controls should be laid down in separate procedures. Responsibility for both data and controls should be clearly allocated. This function is finally responsible for the completeness and accuracy of the data.

Recruitment of Reliable Personnel

Although the recruitment of personnel is not a classic internal control measure, it is beyond doubt that this measure is one of the most important steps in mitigating operational risk. Good, loyal and reliable personnel who are highly involved will try to eliminate error sources and will continuously improve the procedures they are responsible for. The recruitment of reliable personnel is possible after fulfilling the following criteria:

- Background scanning when hiring for sensitive positions.
- Checks of references.
- Interviews conducted by well-experienced staff, with the interview not only focusing on the candidate's knowledge, but also on his background, interests, behaviour and ethical values.
- During the interviews, interviewers should also register the non-verbal communications. These often indicate more about the candidate than he is actually telling.

An investment in a good hiring procedure for new staff and adequate training of employees in interview techniques is a good basis for an adequate control environment.

Conclusion

The internal control measures which have been described are building blocks which can be used by all responsible staff while designing procedures. The design of procedures, however, is an area which should not be underestimated; it requires a sound understanding of the inherent risks in products which need to be controlled. The internal control measures should be used only after due consideration. Too many controls will be uneconomical, since the cost involved may even absorb the full margin of the products.

The measures described should help responsible management to improve the design of procedures and the quality of processing in a financial institution. Although the description of the measures may be clear, it is highly recommended that the available expertise in the organization is fully used. It is better to prevent a wrong design, than to incur a deficit in an existing procedure later on.

RISK TRANSFER

If risk mitigation is not improving the risk potential of the financial institution, the management may consider risk transfer. This is particularly the

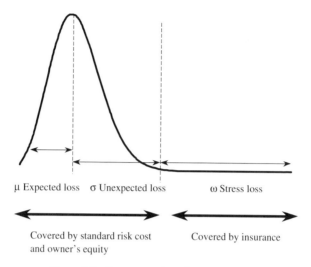

μ Expected loss   σ Unexpected loss   ω Stress loss

Covered by standard risk cost   Covered by insurance
and owner's equity

Figure 3.8   Representation of operational risk

case in the area 'high severity – low frequency' which can be explained with reference to Figure 3.8.

The following possibilities of risk transfer are available to financial institutions at this moment (March 2001):

- Outsourcing
- Insurances

  - fidelity insurance
  - electronic computer crime insurance
  - professional indemnity
  - directors' and officers' insurance
  - legal expense insurance
  - stockbrokers' indemnity
  - unauthorized trading insurance
  - banker's blanket bond
  - property insurance
  - FIORI

Outsourcing enables a financial institution to improve the quality of their processing if the institution is not able to adequately invest in processing capacity. New products in particular need the attention of operations management, since they become more and more complex. For example structured products cannot be processed by straight-through processing applications. Outsourcing, however, reduces the dependency on key staff.

It should be noted that outsourcing does not fully transfer the operational risk from the financial institution to the outsourcing partner. Senior management of the financial institution is still fully responsible for the outsourcing activities to the supervisor, and the outsourcing partner will not bear any reputational losses caused by low-quality processing. The financial institution has to cope with customer complaints caused by poor processing, since the customers will hold the financial institution completely responsible for any resulting damages. The loss of customers may occur in an extreme situation.

These remarks should, however, not be seen as a reason not to use outsourcing. Outsourcing may be quite useful, especially if the financial institution is not able to hold the necessary qualified resources (both human and system resources). The financial institution, however, should make sure that the service-level agreement includes arrangements regarding management information about the processing quality, and clear escalation procedures in the case of errors or differences in opinion regarding the solution of problems that might occur. Senior management of the financial institution should have the capacity to give direct orders to the outsourcing partner in order to meet the supervisory requirements.

Fidelity insurance gives cover against dishonest or fraudulent actions of employees. Damages to offices and some forms of trading losses may also be covered. This insurance normally does not cover against external criminal activities, especially in the case of hacking.

Electronic computer crime insurance covers computer operations, the damages caused by viruses, and damages caused during electronic communication. Today the risks in e-commerce should also be considered. In this case 'spoofing' is particularly mentioned; the financial institution's web site is misused by foreign frames in which the user is requested to enter account numbers, credit card numbers and so on, which are then misused by the third party intruder. The user may trust the question, since he thinks it is the financial institution requiring the information.

Professional indemnity insurance covers mainly errors caused by poor advice. As described in Chapter 2, poor advice may cause customer complaints which can end in court. Since the financial institution will be held liable for the consequences of poor advice, the damage amount may be quite high.

Directors' and officers' insurance covers the expenses of both directors and officers as a consequence of legal actions regarding the performance of their official duties. Officers and directors are held personally liable for the company's loss by, for example, shareholders. The insurance protects the private assets of directors and officers in the event of legal action.

Legal expense insurance covers the cost of legal actions such as court expenses, lawyers' bills and expenses incurred in obtaining expert opinions to prove the financial position.

Stockbrokers' indemnity insurance covers the financial institution against damages caused by, for example, neglecting exchange rules; but also in the case of forgery or dishonesty by employees.

Unauthorized trading insurance proved its importance in the Leeson case, in which rogue trading cost Barings Bank its very existence. The insurance covers the financial institution for the consequences of unauthorized trading.

Bankers' blanket bond covers loss of money, securities or other negotiable instruments accepted for cash as part of the usual cheque-cashing operation. It does not intend to cover other fidelity or crime exposures that may arise from other operations on the same or other premises. The intended operations are those that cash cheques and other negotiable instruments, such as money orders, food stamps and travellers' cheques, for a fee. No coverage is afforded for such risks as non-sufficient fund checks, which are considered a business risk in this type of operation, or fraudulent items.

Property insurance covers the bank against a loss of their property caused, for example, by fire, flood or terrorism.

FIORI (financial institutions operational risk insurance) is a new product issued by Swiss Re. It has a big advantage in that it includes operational risk causes, instead of excluding such risks as is common in other policies. This insurance only becomes of interest, of course, if the decrease in market value is larger than the premium to be paid.

The insurance contains the following benefits for financial institutions:

- The profit and loss account is not affected by the insured loss amount.
- The liquidity position of the financial institution is not influenced by an operational loss.
- The owners' equity position of the bank does not change and therefore the bank's rating is not affected.
- The bank's management can concentrate on business issues instead of solving the bank's liquidity needs.

The following risks are covered by the *FIORI* insurance:

- Liability
  - Each loss as a result of neglecting legal obligations by the financial institution or one of its subsidiaries, its management or staff

members, its representatives or companies to which the financial institution has outsourced.

    o Fines are not excluded from the coverage.

- Fidelity and unauthorized activities

    o Dishonesty is broadly defined in the insurance policy.
    o All trading business is covered.
    o Potential income has not been excluded from the coverage.
    o Repair costs are also covered.

- Technology risks

    o Sudden and irregular failure of own-built applications is covered.
    o Normal processing errors and millennium problems are excluded from the insurance coverage.

- Asset protection

    o All risks concerning buildings and property are covered.
    o The coverage includes both own and trust assets.

- External fraud

    o Coverage for external fraud is broadly defined.
    o The coverage includes not only existing customers.
    o Potential income is also not excluded in this case.

It can be seen that the coverage of this operational risk insurance is quite broad; the product sets a high standard in the insurance market. The coverage, however, is accompanied by considerable requirements, which are expressed in a high minimum access point and high premiums. The minimum access point (retention amount) amounts to US$100 000 000 for each and every loss claim. This is a high amount which cannot easily be absorbed by financial institutions, particularly small ones. Such institutions would become bankrupt even after insurance coverage. The premium is expected to be between 3 per cent and 8 per cent of the amount covered. Target clients for the insurance company should have balance sheet totals of at minimum US$20 billion. If a risk volume of US$100 million is insured, the premium would be between US$3 million and US$8 million. Even these amounts cannot be absorbed by small financial institutions.

Moreover the following requirements have to be fulfilled by the financial institutions:

- The insurance is only offered to financial institutions domiciled in Western Europe, North America, Australasia, Hong Kong, Singapore and Israel.
- The gross earnings from insurance business should not contribute more than 50 per cent to the financial institution's total gross earnings.
- The financial institution should be listed on an Exchange.
- A risk review including an extensive application form is required.

In case of a loss, the insurance company buys shares of the financial institution, which solves two problems:

- The acute liquidity problem is solved, since the credit lines of the financial institution will be immediately frozen after a big operational loss.
- The solvency ratio of the bank and the BIS ratio are not heavily affected.

Especially in the case of the current insurance market, self-insurance may be a good alternative. The possibilities described by Marshall (2001)[10] are:

- Using internal funds
- Establishing lines of credit
- Raising external funds
- Using a captive insurer

Some financial institutions have large positions in current or financial assets, which can easily be liquidated. In the case of a manifest operational risk the financial institution can bear the risk itself by liquidating these assets. A manifest operational risk mostly does not cause a solvency risk in the first place, but a liquidity risk; the financial institution is then able to cushion this risk itself.

Establishing lines of credit is normally only feasible for 'sunny days'. As soon as the financial institution is confronted by an acute operational risk, its credit lines will be frozen. Since larger losses are being discussed here, the benefits of these kind of credit lines should not be overestimated; premiums will be quite high and a near default case may cause the creditor to freeze the credit line as well.

What is true for the credit line is even more true for raising external funds after the loss. It will be quite hard for the financial institution to find somebody willing to lend money under such critical circumstances. The way FIORI functions may be seen as raising external funds as well, since the insurer buys stock and gives liquidity.

The last possibility is a *captive insurance*. A captive company is normally fully-owned by the financial institution and located offshore, since the regulatory requirements are quite moderate and the tax benefits considerable. It allows the financial institution to set the premium paid for their tax position, and the tax rules for insurers allow deduction of the discounted value of the incurred losses. Moreover a captive insurance company allows direct access to the reinsurance market.

A captive company is sometimes held by more than one financial institution. Such a so-called risk-retention company has some benefits for financial institutions:

- Lower rates
- Faster pay outs
- Broader coverage

It may be concluded that the possibilities for transferring operational risk are not fully developed at this moment. It is expected that the instruments will be improved in the coming years, especially if the regulatory treatment of risk transfers is clarified.

MANAGEMENT INFORMATION

Since operational risk is such an important theme for financial institutions, it should be included within the management information. Information concerning operational risk is not only justified by the regulatory capital charge; senior management should document the controls regarding the quality of the organization. Management needs to make a report in the financial statement regarding the quality of the organization, which is to be audited by the external auditor.

Operational risk management means that senior management should at least have room to manoeuvre before the risk becomes manifest. Management is therefore interested in risk indicators, which should predict an upcoming risk. At this moment the theory regarding risk indicators is not proven. Theoretical frameworks fail and research is needed at that time to find out if the indicators highly correlate with the losses which resulted from the risks the financial institution was exposed to.

As long as a structural approach fails, the information collected in the quick scan may be helpful as management information. This information also discloses potential operational risks. If the processing capacity is almost completely used, management should be aware of possible problems in case of increasing processing demands. It is better to increase the processing capacity before the system fails and the financial institution is faced with claims from counterparties and clients. The same is true for an increasing number of nostro items. It is better to switch capacity to improve the poor situation, than to wait for the first problems which may have a considerable impact on the financial institution's profit and loss account.

The possibility of retrieving information from the systems may be a limiting factor for the supply of management information. In some cases it is hard to derive sufficient information to support a regular management information cycle. On the other hand, management should sometimes insist on information from their staff members, since reasons for non-delivery are sometimes used without a real basis. A proposal for regular management information regarding operational risk is included in Appendix 3.

Information regarding the quantification of operational risk and the resulting capital allocation should also be included in the management information. As discussed in Chapter 1, the financial institution's capital is a scarce resource which should be carefully managed. Moreover, the regulatory capital used to cover operational risk is actually 'dead capital', since it cannot be used to underlie transactions which contribute to the bank's income.

Contrary to the capital used for credit and market risk, the required return on the capital for operational risk also has to be earned by other products, since the investment of the owners' equity will not meet the return requirements set by the managing board in order to meet the shareholders' requirements as well. It is therefore very important that management receives the necessary information on time in order to take decisions on trends in the financial institution's risk exposure, which would unnecessarily increase the regulatory capital charge for operational risk.

FUTURE TRENDS

At this moment (March 2001) our understanding of operational risk is not fully developed. The regulatory discussion has been more intense since the Basle Committee issued its Consultative Paper, and the consulting period ends at 31 May 2001. At this moment financial institutions are researching the implications of the new capital accord for the regulatory capital charge. This research is only partly possible, however, since data from a sample of banks is needed to calculate the effects of the standard and internal measurement approaches.

Secondly, most financial institutions are now heavily involved in performing a health check regarding the mentioned qualifying criteria for both the standardized and internal measurement approaches. The loss-collection theme is still a considerable issue in most financial institutions. Discussions have also started on the handling of external data and the necessary set up of data consortia, which function as trustees for the member banks. Anonymity is an important issue here which should be quickly solved. Financial institutions are going to deliver very sensitive information to third parties and they therefore need to be absolutely sure that nobody (also the trustee) is able to trace the information back to each individual financial institution. Consultants also should not be allowed to benefit from the data collection by selling benchmarking to other financial institutions. It would therefore be a good alternative to ask a governmental or supra-national institution to act as trustee for the loss information.

An issue which should be clarified is the consideration of risk transfer measured for the calculation of the regulatory capital charge. Although the Basle Committee has no objections in principle against a consideration of transfer measures, the exact impact is still unclear. One could probably say that the coverage amount can be added to the guarantee capital of the financial institution as long as the payment in the case of a manifest operational risk is certain. The addition, however, should only be allowed if the current guarantee capital of the financial institution exceeds the retention amount as mentioned in the insurance policy. Otherwise the financial institution would be faced with bankruptcy, since the owners' equity would be negative even after the insurance payment.

Financial institutions will also need to cope with the optimization of the regulatory capital charge. Although internal models are not allowed in the first phase, the development of such models will take place. Both the financial industry and the researchers involved are now challenged by the requirement to design a model which not only includes direct losses, but is also able to properly handle reputational risks and losses.

4 Concluding Remarks

It is fair to say that both practice and science are still seeking to find a proper method to control and manage operational risks in financial institutions. Nevertheless, important progress has been made in recent years. The emphasis, however, is probably too much on the quantification of the operational risk exposure. Certainly the quantification of operational risk in financial institutions is an important issue which has to be satisfactorily solved not only for regulatory capital charge purposes, but it should be kept in mind that the management of operational risks is not necessarily helped by a quantification of the operational risk exposure. The management and control of the operational risks should have the highest priority within financial institutions and with regulators. Management and control may be better served by qualitative impressions rather than sophisticated statistical analysis. Expert judgement regarding the risk potential and probability may be a valuable approach as well, since so many factors play an important role that in the short term no sound scientific approach is to be expected.

The regulatory discussion has not yet been concluded. It is expected that the Basle Committee will address the issues brought forward by the various financial institutions and banking associations. At this moment the Basle Committee is conducting a quantitative impact study regarding the proposals. The results are important to individual financial institutions since determining factors for the regulatory capital charge need to be delivered by the supervisor. At this moment the financial institutions do not know exactly which banks are part of the so-called bank's sample, which will be used for the determination of the β-factor in the standardized approach and the exposure indicator and the γ-factor in the internal measurement approach. Financial institutions can only guess the regulatory capital charge regarding operational risk. It is quite clear that both experts and management see themselves confronted with a sub-optimal situation, since management cannot anticipate the effects of the regulatory capital charge which will be definitely implemented in the year 2004. Most internationally operating financial institutions will not be allowed to use the basic indicator approach as long as their domicile is in the European Union.

It is expected that scientific efforts regarding models and the predictive quality of key risk indicators will be firmed up after the final proposal of the Basle Committee. Management of risk mainly focuses on risk mitigation and therefore early warning signals will become the most important part of operational risk management.

Progress regarding management, control and quantification of operational risk can be greatly assisted by open discussions of practitioners about their successes and issues. I would be grateful if you the reader would contribute by sharing your ideas, successes and issues with me, to allow us to research in such a way that together we all take the quality of operational risk management and control one step forward.

Appendix 1   Operational Risk: Diagnosis

Process
Assessed by:
Date:

Category	Question	Assessment				Comments
		4	3	2	1	
		very good	*good*	*satisfactory*	*poor*	
General controls	Access					
	Are hardware rooms only accessible by authorized staff members?					
	Is a security officer appointed and are his duties and responsibilities clearly described in a job description?					
	Is the password of the system administrator divided between two staff members?					
	Can it be assumed that staff members keep their passwords secret?					
	Are visitors accompanied to the hardware room?					
	Is a firewall implemented in the case of external communication?					
	Can only known IP addresses pass the firewall?					

General controls		
		Is the check of the authenticity of third parties which communicate with the bank ensured?
		Are system administrators enabled to manipulate data without using the corresponding application?
		Are the system administrators recorded in a journal which cannot be influenced by these system administrators?
		Are user-ids of staff members who have resigned deleted on time?
		Are used-ids of staff members who are absent for a longer time disabled?
		Are wrong log-ons recorded in a journal and checked by the security officer?
		Are only the functions enabled which are necessary for a staff member's function?
		Are the access rights reviewed if a staff member is appointed to another job in the bank?
		Are sensitive data transmitted only via secure pathways?
		Are critical data encrypted during the transmission?
	Access	
	Overall rating	
	Change management	Is a change management procedure available?
		Are responsibilities clearly defined in the change management procedure?
		Are system tests planned?

Appendix 1 *continued*

Category	Question	Assessment				Comments
		4 *very good*	*3* *good*	*2* *satisfactory*	*1* *poor*	
	Are integration tests planned?					
	Are user acceptance tests planned?					
	Are standard tests with expected results available?					
	Are standard tests regularly reviewed and are new products added and included in the expected results?					
Change management Overall rating					■	
Capacity management	Is capacity management of systems decribed in a procedure?					
General controls	Are the available network, hard disk and processor capacities continually monitored at least for all critical systems?					
	Are the capacity management systems intelligent, e.g. do they create band widths and do they warn the system administrators as soon as an excess of band width is threatened? Are warnings recorded and brought					

to the attention of the IT management?

	Capacity management / Overall rating	
General controls	Backup/ recovery	Is a list of business-critical systems available?
		Is a deputy available in case decisions regarding recovery measures need to be taken?
		Is a detailed recovery procedure available which describes the necessary steps after a system breakdown?
		Are critical systems doubled?
		Are critical systems connected to two independent power systems?
		Are communication connections for critical systems arranged over two different carriers?
		Are the production and recovery systems clustered in such a way, that the backup system can replace the production system immediately after a system break down?
		Is data stored on external backup devices and stored outside the main building?
		Are recovery procedures periodically tested?
	Backup/ recovery Overall rating	

Appendix 1 *continued*

Category	Question	Assessment 4 *very good*	3 *good*	2 *satisfactory*	1 *poor*	Comments
General controls	Emergency plan	Has an emergency plan been developed for all critical systems?				
		Are communication lines and responsibilities clearly defined in the emergency plan?				
		Is the emergency plan tested periodically?				
		Is change management of the emergency procedure guaranteed in such a way that all changes in processes and systems are considered?				
	Emergency plan Overall rating				■	
Human resources	Recruitment	Are the required qualifications clearly formulated for each job?				
		Are the applicant's qualifications clearly matched with the required qualifications as decribed in the job description?				
		Is a recruitment procedure available?				
		Are the applicant's documents randomly checked?				
		Is a statement certifying 'good conduct' required for critical positions?				

Human resources	Recruitment Overall rating	■ Are the personal features of the applicant assessed in the interview (e.g. Does the applicant fit in the team?)?
	Knowledge	■ Is a required knowledge profile for each job position available? Is continuing education of staff members guaranteed by a corresponding procedure? Is a rotation plan for the staff members in the department available? Is new knowledge (like new products, processes, etc.) clearly explained in departmental meetings? Is knowledge-sharing stimulated by management (both in the department and between departments)?
	Knowledge Overall rating	
Human resources	Appraisal	Do management and staff members agree upon targets which should be realized within a certain timeframe? Are targets realistically formulated (especially sales budgets and project targets)? Do both managers and staff members discuss progress on a regular basis? Are actions following discussions registered and followed up?

Appendix 1 *continued*

Category	Question	Assessment				Comments
		4 *very good*	*3* *good*	*2* *satisfactory*	*1* *poor*	
Appraisal Overall rating	Is remuneration transparently organized: e.g. does a causal relationship between salaries and achieved results exist?				■	
Human resources	Desk organization/conduct					
	Is the desk provided with the necessary systems?					
	Is a backup of key staff members organized and are the backup staff authorized with all the necessary authorities?					
	Is the environment motivating?					
	Have the staff members a good relationship between each other?					
	Is the workload allocation over the available staff members well-organized?					
	Is much overtime necessary?					
	Are holidays so planned that all necessary activities can be carried out?					
	Is the illness rate normal for the size of the department?					
	Is the ratio between permanent staff members and temps acceptable?					

Desk organization/conduct
Overall rating ■

Human resources — Exit interviews

Are exit interviews conducted if staff members have resigned?
Are the results of the interviews analysed?
Are adjustments planned and is the implementation of these adjustments followed up?

Exit interviews
Overall rating ■

Management — Code of conduct

Is a code of conduct available regarding the desired moral and ethical behaviours in the company?
Is this code of conduct discussed with the employees?
Do the staff members know which behaviour is acceptable and which actions should be taken if they are confronted with unacceptable behaviour?
Do senior management support ethically and morally correct behaviour by giving the right examples themselves?
Do both management and staff members adhere to the code of conduct?

Appendix 1 *continued*

Category	Question	Assessment				Comments
		4 *very good*	3 *good*	2 *satisfactory*	1 *poor*	
Code of conduct Overall rating		■				
Management Management behaviour	Does management seriously follow up signals indicating undesired behaviour and does it take corrective actions?					
	Is misbehaviour of third parties corrected (e.g. bribery)?					
	Are disciplinary actions carried out by management in the case of misbehaviour?					
	Has management communicated the consequences of an unauthorized limit excess?					
	Are management interventions in normal procedures avoided as much as possible?					
	Is the suspension of internal control measures separately documented and approved (e.g. in the case of a system constraint)?					
Management behaviour						

■

Management	Overall rating	
	Board of directors	Do the non-voting members of the board of directors act independently from voting members?
		Are the non-voting members on the board experts on the activities of the company?
		Has the chief internal auditor unlimited access to the chairman of the board of directors?
		Is the board of directors informed about achieved business results completely, accurately and on time?
		Is an audit and compliance committee installed, which is chaired by the chairman of the board?
	Board of directors	
	Overall rating	

■

Management	Management style	Is management acting in a risk-sensitive manner?
		Is the staff turnover in important audit, accounting or operations functions in line with the turnover in the industry?
		Does management use the control function to direct the bank according to the strategy?
		Are the valuation rules chosen in accordance with the business of the bank (no window dressing)?

130

Appendix1 *continued*

Category	Question	Assessment				Comments
		4 *very good*	3 *good*	2 *satisfactory*	1 *poor*	
	Does confidential information at management level remain confidential?					
	Do the various management levels discuss the bank's strategy and the tactical consequences?					
	Does management focus on long-term effects while taking decisions?					
Management style						
Overall rating					■	
Management Organization	Does the organization structure fit the bank's activities?					
	Is authority properly delegated and controlled?					
	Has management enough knowledge to control the delegated authorities effectively?					
	Is management periodically informed regarding delegated authorities?					
Organization Overall rating					■	

Process	General	Are the requirements for processes clearly defined?	
		Is an approval process implemented in which senior management, the controller and the internal audit department are involved?	
		Are responsibilities and authorities clearly defined in the processes?	
	General Overall rating		■
Process	Internal controls	Has a risk analysis regarding processes and products been conducted?	
		Are the identified risks mitigated by the implementation of adequate internal control measures?	
		Are the internal control measures automated?	
		In case of error detection by an internal control measure, is the correction phase descripted in the process?	
		Are the detected errors recorded and are the causes of these errors analysed?	
	Internal controls Overall rating		■
Process	Segregation of duties	Are segregation of duties included in the processes at the right points?	
		Are segregation of duties supported by the IT systems (e.g. general controls)?	
		Could one assume that the segregation of duties functions in reality?	

Appendix 1 *continued*

Category	Question	Assessment				Comments
		4 *very good*	3 *good*	2 *satisfactory*	1 *poor*	
Segregation of duties Overall rating					■	
Suspense accounts	Is a process implemented regarding the opening, handling and closure of suspense.					
	Are new suspense accounts only opened in the case of real necessity?					
	Is the responsibility for a suspense account clearly assigned to a staff member?					
	Are balances on the suspense accounts specified on a regular basis (at least once a month)?					
	Are these specifications checked and signed off by the responsible managers?					
	Are these specifications checked as to accuracy by the accounting department?					
	Does the accounting department pay attention to the 'refreshment' of old items by posting them from one suspense account to another?					

Process

	■ Are the open items aged and the old open items followed up with special attention by both management and the accounting department?
Suspense accounts	
Overall rating	
Process	
Nostro accounts	Is a process implemented indicating with which banks nostro accounts can be opened?
	Are nostro accounts assigned to an account manager who negotiates the conditions on a regular basis?
	Is the reconciliation between the internal account and the external statements of account implemented outside the departments which can directly authorize payments charged to these accounts?
	Does the bank receive statements of account per SWIFT (MT950) and is the reconciliation executed automatically?
	Are the matching criteria entered in the matching system by staff members who are not themselves responsible for the reconciliations?
	Are the matching criteria so implemented that larger items cannot be reconciled wrongly (at least reference, value date and amount should match)?

134

Appendix 1 *continued*

Category	Question	Assessment				Comments
		4 very good	3 good	2 satisfactory	1 poor	
	Is the nostro account reconciliation performed on a daily basis?					
	Are open items sent to the responsible departments and is proper processing monitored?					
	Are the open items regularly analysed and aged? Is this information sent to the responsible management?					
	Is the relationship between the throughput on the accounts and the open items acceptable?					
	Is a separate loss account for interest claims implemented and are the items duly analysed?					
	Is the necessity of each nostro account reviewed on a regular basis?					
Nostro accounts Overall rating				■		

Appendix 2 Operational Risk: Error Trees

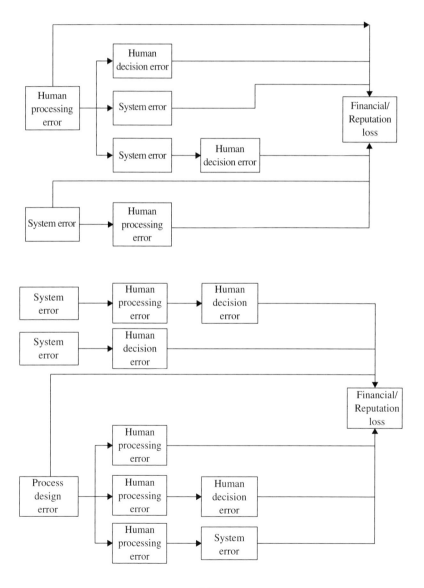

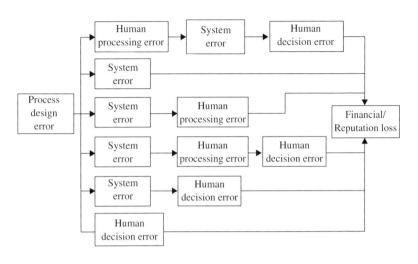

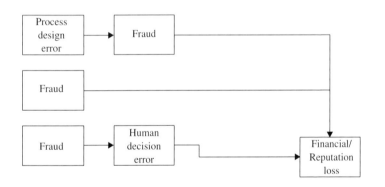

Appendix 3   Transaction Volume

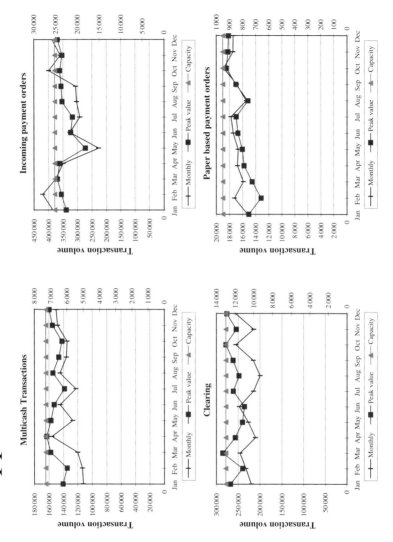

Open items per currency

Currency	Correspondent bank	Number of open items	Value of open items
GB£	National Westminster	12	1. 256.870
euro	Landeszentralbank	29	12. 589.654
US$	J.P. Morgan	11	10. 254.789
Total open items		52	

Number of open items as per 31 August 2000

Product	<5 days	6–15 days	16–31 days	>31 days	Sum	Jul. 00	Jun. 00	May 00
FX-forward	4	5			9	7	5	5
Loans	5	9	3		17	15	13	10
Derivatives	2	8	8		18	12	9	6
Deposits	7	1			8	6	3	1
Total open items	18	23	11	0	52	40	30	22

Value of the open items euro 000s	<5 days	6–15 days	16–31 days	>31 days	Sum	Jul. 00	Jun. 00	May 00
General ledger debit balances	3285	750			4035	7	5	5
Statement credit balances	604	1000	750		2354	15	13	10
General ledger credit balances	3245	120	200		3565	12	9	6
Statement debit balances	104	200	166		470	6	3	1

Nostro Reconciliation

Credit items

Account	Value (euro 000s)	Number of open items					
		Sum of the open items	*0–1 day*	*2–5 days*	*5–15 days*	*16–31 days*	*>31 days*
Amounts to be paid	1 235	3	1	1	1		
Deutsche Börse Clearing AG	12 458	200	180	20			
Sum	13 693	203	181	21	1	0	0
Debit items							
Amounts to be paid	120	4	3	1			
Deutsche Börse Clearing AG	3 350	56	45	11			
Sum	3 470	60	48	12	0	0	0

Analysis of Open Items on Nostro Accounts

Reconciliations

Reconciliation	Product group	Value	Amount System 1	Amount System 2	Clarified differences	Unclarified differences	Comments
Position reconciliation							
Front office system/ Back office system	Equity cash	euro	2 562 407	2 559 807	3		Error was corrected next day
P&L reconciliation							
Front office system/ Back office system	Derivatives	euro	450 213	468 752	1		Wrong rate of exchange for US $ was used
Custody reconciliation							
Deutsche Börse Clearing/ Back office system	Equity cash	euro	214 520	214 520			

Confirmations

Open confirmations per product

Product	Aug. 00	Jul. 00	Jun. 00
FX-forward	8	5	4
Loans	9	5	3
Forward rate agreements	5	3	2
Over the counter options	1	1	1
Sum	23	14	10

Open confirmations (aged)

Product	<5 days	6–15 days	16–31 days	32–60 days	>60 days
FX-forward	3	5			
Loans	1	5	3		
Forward rate agreements	3	2			
Over the counter options	1				
Sum	8	12	3	0	0

Confirmations (Value)

Value of the confirmations per product

Product	Aug. 00	Jul. 00	Jun. 00
FX-forward	2000	500	450
Loans	900	500	350
Forward rate agreements	500	300	250
Over the counter options	100	125	100
Sum	3500	1425	1150

Value of the confirmations per product

Product	<5 days	6–15 days	16–31 days	32–60 days	>60 days
FX-forward	1200	800			
Loans	100	500	300		
Forward rate agreements	300	200			
Over the counter options	100				
Sum	1700	1500	300	0	0

Interest Claims*

Description	Value (*euro 000s*)	Number of claims	<5 days	5–15 days	16–31 days	>31 days
Our open claims with third parties						
Open claims of third parties with us						

Claims older than 30 days should be specified in detail.
* No actual figures within the table, as in the original document.

Open Audit Items

Department	Audit report date	Audit finding	Completion date	Management comments
Settlement	31 July 2000	Confirmations are not matched in time	31 August 2000	This issue should be addressed with the front office as well, since the counterparties do not send their confirmations on time

Suspense Accounts

Complaint category	Number of complaints		
	Aug. 00	Jul. 00	Jun. 00
Payment was credited to the wrong account	15	10	8
Payment was executed late	7	5	3
Payment was wrongly routed	4	3	2

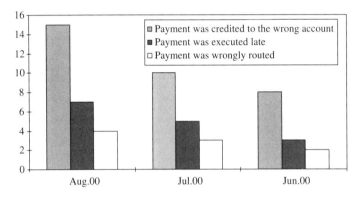

Analysis of the customer's complaints

Appendix 4 Loss Factor Categorization

Tier 1	Tier 2	Tier 3	Explanation/examples
People	Employee fraud/ malice (criminal)	Collusion	Involves more than one person, at least one of whom is an employee
		Embezzlement	Obtaining money by deception; employee effectively steals from a client/customer e.g. raising false loans, altering cheques
		(Deliberate) sabotage of bank reputation	
		(Deliberate) money laundering	
		Theft – physical	e.g. computer equipment, cash, artwork
		Theft – intellectual property	e.g. deliberate theft of software
		Programming fraud	e.g. deliberate introduction of a computer virus by an employee
		Other	
	Unauthorized activity / rogue trading / employee misdeed	Misuse of privileged information	e.g. insider trading, front running
		Churning	Falsely inflating a deal for commission purposes
		Market manipulation	False/misleading statements; price manipulation
		Activity leading to deliberate mispricing	Unauthorized or other irregular activity which affects internal portfolio pricing
		Activity with unauthorized counterparty	
		Activity in unauthorized product	
		Limit breach	Deliberate breach by employee
		Incorrect models (intentional)	Deliberately manipulating model; unauthorized changes to parameters

	Activity outside exchange rules Illegal/aggressive selling tactics Ignoring / short-circuiting procedures (deliberate) Other	Deliberately or negligently selling inappropriate product or dispensing incorrect advice
Employment law	Wrongful termination Discrimination / equal opportunity Harassment Non-adherence to other employment law Non-adherence to Health and Safety regulations Other	
Workforce disruption	Industrial action Other	By firm's employees
Loss or lack of key personnel	Lack of suitable employees Loss of key personnel Other	Suitable employees not available internally or in marketplace when needed This may result in a loss of clients / business or the loss of a product line
Process Payment / settlement delivery risk	Failure of / inadequate internal payment/settlement process Losses through reconciliation failure Securities delivery errors Limit breach	*Not* due to IT system failure. Note that breakdown of IT system should be reported under systems failure (systems failure) As a result of inadequate internal processes or employee error e.g. daylight risk

Appendix 4 *continued*

Tier 1	*Tier 2*	*Tier 3*	*Explanation / examples*
Process		Insufficient capacity of people or systems to cope with volumes Other	Caused by unexpected volumes and/or lack of resource (rather than lack of skills)
	Documentation or contract risk	Document not completed properly Inadequate clauses/contract terms Inappropriate contract terms	Includes not adhering to account opening procedures
		Inadequate sales records Failure of due diligence Other	Inadequately documented advice Generally relating to M&A
	Valuation/pricing	Model risk	Failure of model for intrinsic reasons e.g. inappropriate parameters, incorrect programming, invalid assumptions, mathematical errors
		Input error Other	e.g. wrong data, incorrect input, incorrect mark to market
	Internal/external reporting	Inadequate exception reporting Accounting/book-keeping failure/inadequate data Inadequate risk management reporting Inadequate regulatory reporting Inadequate financial reporting Inadequate tax reporting Inadequate stock exchange/ securities reporting Non-adherence to Data Protection	e.g. poor, untimely management information

147

Category	Risk	Notes
Compliance	Act / Privacy Act / similar	
	Other	
	Failure to adhere to internal compliance procedures	
	Failure of external compliance procedures	Excluding failures of reporting identified under internal / external reporting above
	Breach of Chinese walls	
Project risk / change management	Inadequate project proposal/plan	
	New product process inadequacies	Failure to analyse and manage operational risks involved in new products e.g. capacity
	Project overruns	Costs associated with project overruns
	Other	
Selling risks	Inappropriate product selection	
	Product complexity	Product complexity leads to claims from customers who have been unable to understand it
	Poor advice (including securities)	
	Other	
Systems — Technology investment risk	Inappropriate architecture	
	Strategic risk (platform / suppliers)	e.g. IT integration (inherited through merger / take-over) e.g. incorrect decision with respect to build or buy
	Inappropriate definition of business requirements	Not correctly specified; supplier suggests inappropriate system; inadequate functionality
	Incompatibility with existing systems	
	Obsolescence of hardware	
	Obsolescence of software	e.g. supplier no longer supports current version
	Other	
Systems development and implementation	Inadequate project management	
	Cost/time overruns	With respect to implementation

Appendix 4 *continued*

148

Tier 1	Tier 2	Tier 3	Explanation / examples
Systems		Programming errors (internal/ external)	
		Failure to integrate and or migrate with/from existing systems	
		Failure of system to meet business requirements	Either through failure to deliver specified system or through changed business requirements
		Other	
	Systems capacity	Lack of adequate capacity planning	Volume and flexibility
		Software inadequate	
		Other	
	Systems failures	Network failure	
		Interdependency risk	(Of systems)
		Interface failures	
		Hardware failure	
		Software failure	Not to include interface software
		Internal telecommunication failures	
		Other	
	Systems security breach	External security breaches	e.g. breach of firewall
		Internal security breaches	
		Programming fraud	(By third party)
		Computer viruses	
		Other	
External	Legal/public liability	Breach of environmental management	e.g. waste disposal failure; asbestos; contaminated land/polluter
		Breach of fiduciary / agency duty	

Category	Item	Notes
Criminal activities	Interpretation of law	e.g. local authority swaps; new interpretation
	Misrepresentation	
	Other	
	External frauds/cheque fraud/forgery	
	Fraudulent account opening by client	
	Masquerade	Criminal masquerade of a bank or a banking channel
	Blackmail	
	Robberies (+ theft)	
	Money laundering	
	Terrorism/bomb	
	Disruption to business	i.e. victim
	Physical damage to property	Civil disobedience/protests/riots; sabotage of system or service
	Arson	
	Other	Caused by vandalism
Outsourcing/ supplier risk	Bankruptcy of supplier	
	Breach of responsibility (misuse of confidential data)	
	Inadequate contract	
	Breach of service level agreement	Failure to deliver to time, to quality
	Supplier/delivery failure	Failure to deliver
	Inadequate management of suppliers/service providers	May lead to delivery problems/quality problems
	Other	
Insourcing risk	Insourcing failure	Failure of firm as outsourcer for third party to comply with service level agreement

Appendix 4 *continued*

Tier 1	Tier 2	Tier 3	Explanation / examples
External	Disasters and infrastructural utilities failures	Fire	
		Flood	
		Other natural (geological/meteorological)	e.g. earthquake, volcano, hurricane
		Civil disasters	e.g. spills, collisions
		Transport failure	
		Energy failure	
		External telecommunications failure	
		Disruption to water supply	
		Unavailability of building	Denial of access for any other reason; landlord/third-party failure; e.g. asbestos, legionnaire's disease
		Other	
	Regulatory risk	Regulator changes rules in industry/country	
	Political/government risk	War	
		Expropriation of assets	
		Business blocked	
		Change of tax regime	e.g. withholding tax
		Other changes in law	
		Other	

Notes

1 Definition and Dimensions of Operational Risk

1. Global Derivatives Study Group (1993), p. 50.
2. Committee of Sponsoring Organizations of the Treadway Commission (1992).
3. Hoffmann (1989), p. 40.
4. See for example Rolfes (1999), p. 6.
5. This figure was originally drawn by Stefan Kirmße.
6. David Otley (1999) in *Management Accounting Research*, no. 10, pp. 363–82.

2 Risk Identification and Quantification

1. Derrick Ware (1996), pp. 14, 15.
2. MaH (1995), § 4.
3. This figure is taken from Driessen *et al.* (1993), *Operational Auditing, een managementkundige benadering*.
4. Managers often feel that this is the case, since auditors extensively discuss negative audit findings and positive issues are often not noted in audit reports.
5. Walter Keck and Dean Jovic (1999), *Der Schweizer Treuhänder*, October p. 964.
6. Basle Committee (2001), p. 6.
7. *Ibid. Bundesaufsichtsamt für das Kreditwesen* (1995), pp. 14, 15.
8. *Ibid.*, p. 7.
9. An alternative may be VaR.
10. See W. Sharpe (1985), p. 145 ff and R. Brealey and S. Myers (1988), p. 173 ff.
11. For details on the calculation of β refer to R. Brealey and S. Myers (1988), p. 178 ff.
12. Basle Committee (2001), p. 23.
13. A detailed list of the proposed exposure indicators is included in Appendix 5.
14. Robert Ceske, José V. Hernández and Louis M. Sánchez (2000), p. 7.
15. Basle Committee (2001), p. 13.
16. Reinhard Buhr, *Die Bank*, March 2000.
17. Presentation by Dr Agatha Kalhoff, 29 October 1999, Frankfurt am Main.
18. Michel Crouhy, Dan Galai and Robert Mark (1998), p. 59.
19. Hugo Everts (1999), p. 12.
20. Dejan Jovic (1999), p. 121 ff.
21. Christian T. Hille, Christoph Burmeister and Matthias Otto (2000), *Die Bank*, March 2000, p. 190.

3 Management of Operational Risk

1. Basle Committee (2001), p. 5.
2. The European Commission suggests that local governments retain the possibility in national laws to approve the use of internal business lines in combination with own loss data (European Commission, Commission Services, Second

Consultative Document on Review of Regulatory Capital for Credit Institutions and Investment Firms, 2001, p. 41).
3. The Committee on the Financial Aspects of Corporate Governance (1992), p. 3.
4. Basle Committee (2001), p. 4.
5. Kreditwesengesetz (KWG), § 25a.
6. De Nederlandsche Bank (1988).
7. *Ibid.* (1993).
8. The following sources were used for this section: R.W. Starreveld *et al.* (1991), and E.O.J. Jans (1990).
9. Thomas Stewart (1997), p. 96.
10. Christopher Marshall (2001), p. 444.

References

Bundesaufsichtsamt für das Kreditwesen (BAK) (1995) *Mindestanforderungen an das Betreiben von Handelsgeschäften der Kreditinstitute*, Berlin.

Basle Committee on Banking Supervision (1998) *Operational Risk Management*, Basle.

Basle Committee on Banking Supervision (2001) *Consultative Document Operational Risk, Supporting Document to the New Basle Capital Accord*, Basle.

Brink, G.J. van den (2001) *Operational Risk, Wie Banken das Betriebsrisiko beherrschen*, Stuttgart.

Buhr, R. (2000) '*Messung von Betriebsrisiken – ein methodischer Ansatz*', *Die Bank*, March.

Ceske, R., Hernández, J.V. and Sánchez, L.M. (2000) *Quantifying Event Risk: The Next Convergence*, The Journal of Risk Finance, Spring.

Committee on the Financial Aspects of Corporate Governance (Cadbury Committee, 1992) *Report of the Committee on the Financial Aspects of Corporate Governance*, London.

Committee of Sponsoring Organizations of the Treadway Commission (COSO) (1992) *Internal Control – Integrated Framework*, Jersey City.

Crouhy, M., Galai, D. and Mark, R. (1998) *Key Steps in Building Consistent Operational Risk Measurement and Management*, London.

De Nederlandsche Bank (DNB) (1988) *Memorandum omtrent de betrouwbaarheid en continuïteit van de geautomatiseerde gegevensverwerking in het bankwezen*, Amsterdam.

De Nederlandsche Bank (DNB) (1993) *Circulaire Richtlijnen administratieve organisatie bij kredietinstellingen*, Amsterdam.

Driessen, A.J.G., van der Kerk, J.W. und Molenkamp, A. (1993) *Operational Auditing: een managementkundige benadering*, Deventer.

European Commission (2001) Commission Services, *Second Consultative Document on Review of Regulatory Capital for Credit Institutions and Investment Firms*, Brussels.

Everts, H. (1999) *Operational Risk within a RAROC Framework*, ICM Operational Risk Conference, Frankfurt am Main.

Global Derivatives Study Group (1993) *Derivatives: Practices and Principles*, Washington, DC.

Hetzer, J. (2000) '*Böses Erwachen*', *Manager Magazine*, April.

Hille, C.T., Burmester, C. and Otto, M. (2000) '*Modelle zur risikoadjustierten Kapitalallokation*', *Die Bank*, March.

Hoffmann, G.H. (1989) *Tales of Hoffmann, The Experiences of an International Business Investigator*, Amsterdam.

Jans, E.O.J. (1990) *Grondslagen van de administrative organisatie*, Alphen aan den Rijn/Deurne.

Jovic, D. (1999) *Risikoorientierte Eigenkapitalallokation und Performancemessung bei Banken*, Bern.

Kalhoff, A. (1999) *Allocating Capital for Operational Risk*, ICM Operational Risk Conference, Frankfurt am Main.

153

Keck, W. and Jovic, D. (1999) '*Das Management von operationellen Risiken bei Banken*', *Der Schweizer Treuhänder*, October.

Kinsley, S., Rolland, A., Tinney, A. and Holmes, P. (1998) *Operational Risk and Financial Institutions: Getting Started*, London.

Marschall, C. (2001) *Measuring and Managing Operational Risks in Financial Institutions*, Singapore.

Otley, D. (1999) '*Performance Measurement: A Framework for Management Control Systems Research*', *Management Accounting Research*, no. 10.

Rolfes, B. (1999) *Gesamtbanksteuerung*, Stuttgart.

Starreveld, R.W., de Mare, H.B. and Joëls, E.J. (1990) *Bestuurlijke Informatieverzorging, deel 2*, Alphen aan den Rijn/Deurne.

Starreveld, R.W., de Mare, H.B. and Joëls, E.J. (1991) *Bestuurlijke Informatieverzorging, deel 1*, Alphen aan den Rijn/Deurne.

Stewart, T.A. (1997) *Intellectual Capital, The New Wealth of Organizations*, London.

Ware, D. (1996) *Basic Principles of Banking Supervision, Handbooks in Central Banking*, no. 7, Centre for Central Banking Studies, Bank of England, London.

Index